ENDORSE

"This book is a powerful gift. Your witness is strong and personal, motivating and inspiring, guiding and giving. It also has the grace of personal struggle and failure. I will probably be reading short bits of it for years as my morning devotional. So far, I am Blessed, Graced, Gifted, Loved, Forgiven and Saved. Thanks for sharing."
   -Dr. Ron Presswood; Houston, Texas

"I think this book is right on. The underlying theme is Spirit-driven but the storytelling and personal side make it fun. I reread your corrections and I think you have a good book. It is Spirit-filled and honest. I look at it as a happy, feel-good read. I enjoyed it and found myself chuckling a bit here and there. I have already given it to a lady who has worked for me for 23 years, she is a Christian and teaches a Bible study. She loved it as well."
   -Dr. Jimmy Hill; Greenville, South Carolina

"I believe that anyone who reads this book who is on the fence with regards to Christianity will be convicted to go one way or the other. Those with eyes that can see will want to deepen their walk with Christ or start it as the case may be. Those whose eyes are shut will probably not make it far into the book. Making the reader take a hard look at where he or she really stands with regards to their faith and their relationship with Christ creates tension and discomfort. I know that this is at least one of your goals and you are very effective in attaining it. Your arguments for a salvation experience and a deeper walk with Christ are compelling and well presented. As more and more Christians feel their faith being threatened, they may make their voices louder. After finishing your book, I definitely feel blessed as well as challenged. Thank you Mark for this gift of your heartfelt thoughts. I count myself blessed for having read it and it will make a difference for this knucklehead."
   -Dr. Ron Bautsch; Conroe, Texas

"After reading the first two chapters of this little book, I found that I needed to resign from three different boards of directors I was serving on! Mark paints a picture of what is truly meaningful from the eternal perspective, which I had not really thought about before.

This book will have you thinking of what you're doing with your life and why you're doing it. I found myself on a path that was not as significant as the one I am on now. Everyone can benefit from reading this book!"

-Dr. Mike Schroeder; Arlington Heights, Illinois

"Outstanding book! Tough love is what the people in America need. It made me truly realize that nothing I do is good enough! Only my love for Jesus Christ will carry me through and you made me understand I was not loving Him 100%. I have already read it twice!"

-Dr. Buddy McClung; Houston, Texas

"In a topsy-turvy world where right has become wrong and political correctness is more about being political than correct, we need some clear direction. Dr. Peters hits the bull's eye in "Which Way Is Up?" In a creative approach to answer this question, Mark is funny, convicting, personally transparent, and 100% biblical. If a spiritual fog has set in on your heart, this book will clear the air!"

-Dr. Jay Gross, Senior Pastor; West Conroe Baptist Church

There is a powerful message in this book – a message that, if taken seriously, will change your life and the lives of others around you. It will challenge you to begin TRULY living the life God created you to live.

-Nancy Crutcher; Conroe, Texas

As an elementary teacher of 22 years, it is ever so easy to see how many of our families today are lost as to "Which Way Is Up?" No doubt the way we see the world determines the way we live, act, and perform our lives. Dr. Peters' book challenges us to review, decide, and choose where we are in our faith. Do we possess and have a genuine encounter and relationship with God through Jesus Christ? With a heart-warming charm and a touch of humor, Dr. Peters tells a story to all whether you are a sinner who has yet to decide where you stand with Christianity or an everyday sinning Christian who needs an ultimate review of his/her commitment to God. Do read this book as the challenges will enhance your ability to discern what really is important in all this chaos and discover the best version of you.

-Cindy Odom; The Woodlands, Texas

WHICH WAY IS UP?

FROM AMONGST ALL
THIS CHAOS!

MARK P. PETERS, D.D.S.

Intermedia Publishing Group

WHICH WAY IS UP?

Published by:
Intermedia Publishing Group, Inc.
P.O. Box 2825
Peoria, Arizona 85380
www.intermediapub.com

ISBN 978-1-935529-39-2

DEDICATION

I dedicate this book to my wife – Keyea. You, Sweetie, are the best gift the Lord has given me on this earth! You complete me by being my "temperer", my staunchest critic, and my absolute best friend I have this side of Heaven! The Lord knew what He was doing when He brought us together on that "Championship blind date!"

As well, I dedicate it to my kids, Kailey and Joseph. Thank you both for being such blessings to your Mom and Me!

Lastly, I dedicate this book to my Lord and Savior – Jesus Christ, Who has blessed me so by having me write this book. My prayer is that it will honor and glorify You – as well as further Your kingdom!

ii

TABLE OF CONTENTS

.

PREFACE

The way this book came about was interesting, to say the least. I truly believe the Lord put it on my heart to write this as He woke me from a nap on a flight to Chicago and told me to write down the title. I wrote it down on a piece of paper while I was still in kind of a "dazed-stupor" (many would say this is the "norm" for me).

Once I had written it down, the next thing I "heard" from Him was: THIS IS THE TITLE – NOW WRITE THE BOOK! Now you don't know me, but I'm like you in a lot of ways. I kind of "pooh-poohed" it and told myself later that trip – He couldn't mean for ME to write a book! Could He?

About a month later, on a ski-trip to Colorado, I found myself having a full day with virtually nothing on my plate, and what did I find myself compelled to do? Sit at my laptop and outline the eleven chapters of the book. I figured, "Okay Lord, You gave me the title, the words in it must be good enough for the chapters You want me to write about it." And then, I put it on the back burner again.

Still, a couple of months later, He nudged me to get back on it and at least get something down on paper. I have a patient, Dr. Fran Brown, who has written several books and I ran my experiences about writing the book past him. Fran has been most helpful and patient in encouraging me to proceed and get this done. "Thank you, Fran!"

Even with his help, I still reached another "stall" and

another "blitzkrieg" year of school for the kids, Bible study, teaching a couples Sunday school class, practicing dentistry, running the business, and making "piles" around the house (which by the way, drives Keyea crazy)....anyway, you get the idea!

Finally, just over a year later, He said to me: GET IT DONE! I started using my quiet time in the morning because the Lord just wouldn't let me alone about it! About 8 weeks later, this book was pretty much done.

Let me say that if there are any errors in theology in this book, it is on my account, not His. I have tried to state the truth, His truth, as accurately as I can, and please understand, I am not a Biblical scholar. I've not attended seminary and I certainly don't claim to have all the answers for everyone. I AM – a knucklehead sinner who was told to write this book and I have been obedient in doing so.

I would like to thank Nancy Crutcher, Dr. Ron Presswood, Dr. Buddy McClung, Dr. Jimmy Hill and others who have read the rough draft manuscript and made helpful suggestions on ways to improve the text. My wife, Keyea, has been extraordinarily helpful to run things past and has been patient with this entire effort, "Thank you, Sweetie!"

Most of all, I thank the Lord Jesus Christ for "saving me from myself, my sins, and death!"

INTRODUCTION

If you had told me twenty years ago that I was going to write a book, I would have told you that you were crazy! Especially a book on each of our walks of faith!

"Okay!" you say, "What's with this title, anyway?" I know, I know, it's seemingly a broad and vague question, but one I feel is at the tip of many of our tongues at any given moment, on any particular day, with any particular issue we are dealing with in our lives. Face it, we are BUSY! Busier than virtually all the people who preceded us on this planet! The problem is, we are busy for a lot of wrong reasons, and with this thought in mind, I would like to share with you some of the observations I have had of many of us "busy little bees!"

Have you ever noticed that you find yourself at the end of the day saying, "Wow, I'm so tired! I know I did a great many deeds today, but I don't feel I've made any headway at all for all the energy expended! What eternal benefit was accomplished with anything I did?"

Truth is, a lot of us are so tired and beaten down at the end of the day that we don't even think to ask the question about eternity. We go to bed, mind racing like a dynamo, get a night of "fitful" sleep, and get up to go through another day of the same mindless blur as the previous one.

Does this sound familiar to you? If it doesn't, stop reading right now, call me on the phone, and let me know your secret, because it sounds like you should be writing this book, not me!

There is a great deal of angst and turmoil going on in people's lives, isn't there? I'm sure you get the same comments from acquaintances as I do: "Man, is this all there is in life?"; or "I'm burning the candle at both ends, in fact, I'm fixing to have to start it up in the middle as well, to get all that I need to get done accomplished!"; or "Mark, I don't have time to even think about doing anything else, other than taking care of my family's needs at home!"

Well, get ready, let's have a heart to heart about why we do the things we do, and whether or not they are meaningful, really, in the grand scheme of things.

CHAPTER 1 - WHICH

"Which" is as good a place as any to get us started on our quest for "which way is up?" It denotes a decision, a choice, doesn't it? I do know I am confronted with decisions that seem to be endless each and every minute of every day in my life – aren't you? Yes, we are busy, but busy at what? After all, we are supposed to be busy, aren't we? Don't we have obligations and decisions we have to make? Sure we do, but who made those obligations and what drives those decisions?

One thing that never ceases to amaze me is the amount of time, dedication, and drive we each have to do "things" that are totally meaningless—really. In the grand plan of His design, if we are truthful with ourselves, how meaningful are the choices and decisions we make? Might a more important question be: "What are we doing with His Son?" That's the question we all ought to be grappling with, not "How am I going to be looked at and perceived if I do this or that?"

I mentioned in the introduction that there is a lot of angst and turmoil in our lives, as well as in the lives of those around us. True, isn't it? The trouble is, how much of that angst and turmoil is truly brought on to us by the world and how much is brought on by ourselves? Most of it seems to be brought on by ourselves…. wouldn't you agree? Look, life is made up of choices, decisions, and questions we may have about those choices and decisions.

I have heard of a study done in 1973 which followed people around during their day and found that, on average, they were faced with 350 decisions each day. They redid the study under the same parameters in 2003 and the number of decisions confronted each day had grown to 3500! And that was before the advent of so much texting, emails, tweeting, and the like. Our lives are on fast-forward on a scale unprecedented in history. This puts us into a mode of "problem-solving" we can't seem to keep up with. So many of our problems can be attributed to our perspective and perception of "Why are we here?"

Now there's a question for you! It was a question I had been struggling with all of my life in some form or fashion, and what was surprising about it, was that I didn't even identify the question until I was in my late twenties. You see, I was searching, but I didn't even know it.

I was born in a small town in the Panhandle of Texas… Sorry… I digress!

I had been to church sporadically during my elementary school days but virtually never darkened the door of a church, save for funerals and weddings, from the time I was 12 until I was 28 years old. It wasn't that I loathed church, I would say it was more that my faith was not a priority and was pretty much non-existent. I was living what I thought was the "good life" and didn't need that "religion stuff."

"Which" involves a choice!

Matthew 6:27 And **which** of you by being anxious can add a *single* cubit to his life's span?

Any and every choice I had made in my life had been mine with absolutely no attention paid to the One I should have been paying attention to. I had just graduated from dental school and didn't have any idea where I was going to go to work. I had thought about possibly going to work with my Dad in his practice in West Texas. But the oil-boom had just gone bust and the town my Dad and my Mom lived in had decreased in population from about 35,000 to 18,000 people since the Air Force base had shut down.

Keyea and I were dating and she, being from East Texas, was reluctant to even consider going out to the desolate area my family was from. That was okay with me; I wasn't sure I wanted to return either. In retrospect, I can see plainly now that the Lord didn't plan on me going back out there to live anyway – at least not up to that point.

It was an anxious time for me because I was confronted with a lot of decisions and was "flying by the seat of my pants" on most of them. Before I graduated, I was enrolled in an elective at the dental school and the instructor invited any of the participants in the class to come to his private practice a couple of blocks away to observe. Guess who was the only one to take him up on it?

In the elective course, he had been describing a different type of dentistry than what I had been exposed to at the school, so I felt intrigued and wanted to see what he was talking about. What I saw was truly interesting, more comprehensive, and thought-provoking. It made me realize there was a whole different type of dentistry out there than I had ever known existed.

The other thing that got my attention was the gentleman who was his partner in the practice. He seemed so confident and caring about people, and his skills were impeccable. The two of them seemed to feel I might be a good "fit" for their business and they offered me an opportunity to come in and associate with them in their practice. That was a pivotal point which set me on a course very different from where I really thought I was going to be going after I got out of school.

There was something very interesting about these two guys I was working with on a daily basis. You see, one was a devout Christian and the other was a pretty "dyed in the wool" atheist. What a dichotomy! What a paradox! You know what this did for me though, it gave me a vision of something I had never really been privy to see before – an "up-close and personal" opportunity to observe two men with totally different perspectives on the world and how they related to it.

One thing I discovered as well was that I was always drawn to the "Christian" guy. There was something about him that made me feel more comfortable and relaxed when I was around him. The way he treated his patients and the staff in the office was vastly different from the other gentleman, and the way they each treated me was different as well.

The partnership dissolved within a year after I started working there. Isn't there something in the Bible about being unequally yoked? The Christian moved to another part of town and bought a practice while I stayed employed at the office with the other dentist to fulfill my two year commitment. I stayed in touch with the ex-partner who left and he invited my then fiancée, Keyea, and me to attend a Christian concert with him, his wife, and some of their friends.

Matthew 27:21 But the governor answered and said to them, "**Which** of the two do you want me to release for you?" And they said, "Barabbas."

It was a Dallas Holm concert and I really didn't want to go; but this guy, Buddy, had done so much to help me and I didn't want to let him down. I said we would go. Remember, I hadn't been to church in years, so if you wanted to say I must have felt like a "fish out of water" you would be extremely accurate. But I went and Keyea agreed to go with me as well. By the way, I would have said I was a Christian at that time, but there was absolutely no evidence that I was following Him at that time in any way.

Before that night, I think I might have been one of those who would have asked for the release of Barabbas along with all the other "heathens;" but at the end of the night I found myself so convicted of my sin and so not wanting to be lost for eternity that I was standing up and walking down to the front to give my life to the One who truly matters. Keep in mind, I was a true knucklehead sinner and I was very good at being one as well.

I bought one of Mr. Holm's records and found myself listening to it over and over and yes, there was a part of one of the songs that portrayed the crowd shouting for the crucifixion of Christ and the release of "Barabbas." I remember tears running down my face while listening to that song thinking of how, through my sins, I had been a part of the "nailing of the nails" in His hands and feet.

How about you? Where do you fit on the canvas of this world? You know, there is no middle ground – you either helped nail the nails or you didn't. Have you ever thought about that? Let me clue you in if there is any confusion on your part, "you helped nail the nails!" I know there are some who would say, "Hey, I had no part in that, don't blame me!" I'm sorry to say it, but it's true, whether we want to admit it or not, we all, as sinners, helped "nail the nails."

"Which" foundation will you build on?

> **John 3:6** That **which** is born of the flesh is flesh, and that **which** is born of the Spirit is spirit.
> ❧

There was a change going on in me and I knew it. It wasn't a huge or massive change, but I could tell I wasn't quite thinking the same way I had before; things were different. Oh, I was still a knucklehead sinner no doubt, but I had a new perspective, and it started to unfold for me each and every day. I had been living my life from a totally secular, fleshly, and worldly perspective. Before that concert, there was no evidence of the presence of the Holy Spirit in the decisions or life choices I was making each day.

> **Acts 4:12** "And there is salvation in no one else; for there is no other name under heaven that has been given among men, by **which** we must be saved."
> ∞

After that night, however, there was a "different" perspective and realization that the Lord was helping me to see things around me from a different viewpoint. I am convinced that the Holy Spirit gave me a concern and purpose for my life and I had a sense that He had a reason for me to be - a job for me to do. Please understand, I have no reason to think that I have any special assignment that is superior to anyone else. I just had a sense that things were not the same and He (Christ) was taking on a more and more important role in my life than He ever had before.

The "flesh" hadn't left me, but there was a "spirit" aspect of my life I had never noticed before. My feeling now is that this was the start of the "sanctification process" for my spiritual life to help me start growing to be less dependent on my self-centered lifestyle and more dependent on His God-centered will for my life.

1 Corinthians 3:11 For no man can lay a

foundation other than the one **which** is
laid, **which** is Jesus Christ.

ᢙᢇᢇ

I had been building my life on the world's definition of
success and not on the Lord's definition. I was building on
the wrong foundation, the temporary and fruitless foundation
that has no eternal value whatsoever. How about you? Which
foundation have you been building on – truly building on –
when you look back at your life? Do you have a lot of "stuff?"
You may have it now, but it won't be with you for the long
haul. Check out the last half of Matthew chapter 7 to see the
two foundations offered to us, along with their results.

I see many around me, myself included at times, who are
so preoccupied with building foundations for any number of
reasons, purposes, and things, most of which do not amount
to a real foundation built on Christ, but on some "trivial"
idol whose foundation will crumble in an instant!

Some of my friends and I met at a dental convention in
Dallas for a weekend to attend some seminars and have an
overall fun time getting back together again. Buddy McClung
had given me a Bible, but I had spent no time in it. I didn't
have time! When the group of us were packing up to leave
the hotel and go our various ways, we were in someone's
hotel room having the usual banter guys have about the
events of the weekend.

I noticed a Gideon Bible sitting on the bedside table and
commented that I had been given a Bible but had not spent
any time in it. Dr. Mark Looney, one of my best friends – ever,

made a comment that changed my life and he doesn't even know it. Mark said, "I'll tell you one thing about that Bible. Whatever you do, don't read the last book in that thing – the book of Revelation."

"Why not?" I said.

"Because it'll scare the hell out of you!" he quipped back. "It is scary what that part of the Bible says – don't read it!"

What did I do when I got back home to Houston? You got it. I started reading the book of Revelation in the Bible Buddy had given me. You can guess what happened next – it scared the hell out of me.

What reading that last book in the Bible did for me was expose me to the fact that I may have been mouthing the words that I was a Christian, but I really didn't know my Lord Jesus Christ well enough to have a relationship with Him. As well, reading Revelation helped me to understand that there were a lot of things I didn't understand or know about the God I said I worshiped. As it says in **Revelation 1:3 Blessed is he who reads and those who hear the words of the prophecy, and heed the things which are written in it; for the time is near.**

The time is near......what time is near? I wanted to find out what was near and what this time was, so I started studying that Bible in order to learn about my Lord and see what He wanted me to do with my life – which I owed totally to Him by the way. This started me building on the right foundation – Jesus Christ's.

Galatians 2:20 "I have been crucified with Christ; and it is no longer I who live, but Christ lives in me; and the *life* **which** I now live in the flesh I live by faith in the Son of God, who loved me, and delivered Himself up for me.

∽⁊

If we are to build on the one true foundation, it must be the foundation that will last and is not capable of being chipped away by anything. That foundation is Christ and Him alone. He paid the consummate price, the ultimate sacrifice for all of our sins. We, in turn, must be crucified with Him, say NO to the world, and YES to Him. Have you been crucified with Him? What does it mean to do so? It is hard for us to imagine or even contemplate "dying to self" isn't it? After all, that's not what we are inundated with in the egocentric, self-centered, "go for the gusto" society we live in.

Throughout this book, we will be exploring this doctrine of faith that is so very important to our truly growing in our Lord and in our faith. Yes, we must, as John stated, become less - and He (Christ) more. We must become less "self-centered" and more "God-centered/other-centered" - just as Jesus did for us.

Let me ask you a question: How "self-centered" was Jesus Christ? Show me - nowhere, that I can find. When we look at Him in the Scriptures, He was all about serving His fellow man and His Father. What an example, what a standard, what love He exhibits to us all! And what obedience He showed to His Father! If you want to read about it, just go to Philippians chapter 2 and a multitude of other places in His Word.

"Which" life will you live?

> **Ephesians 2:10** - For we are His workmanship, created in Christ Jesus for good works, **which** God prepared beforehand, that we should walk in them.
>
> ∾

Why are you here? What is your purpose for being? A lot of people I come across in my average day don't seem to have a clue or even think of the question... and I think it's a profound one, that we all should be asking ourselves, everyday.

You know, we have a choice. That's called "freewill" by some or "man's responsibility" by others; and we all seem to have been given a decision to make in this regard. I think part of the problem is that many do not even ask the question. We get so wrapped up in our societal madness that we become totally oblivious to the real reason we were created. And what is this great and meaningful "job" that we are to do?

I was at a family Christian camp in Montana a short while ago, and a lovely gentleman named Larry Moyer, who has a heart for evangelism and knows his purpose, made a statement that hit me between the eyes. He said, "You know there's only one thing you can take to heaven.... a friend!" I can't think of a better way to put it. It's not about being a better you, it's not about health, wealth, and prosperity! Listen, we're playing for keeps here!

This is not a flash in the pan deal! This is ETERNITY with ETERNAL ramifications we have to be thinking about! If we have a Savior and truly love Him, why are we not shouting at the top of our lungs about Him to everyone we come into contact with?

Do you know why? One of the main reasons is PRIDE. You know the kind of pride I'm talking about – that little twinge of a feeling that we are the best at knowing what we need – not some guy who lived 2000 years ago or his Dad either.

I've heard people say, "By the way, that Bible was written so long ago, I'm not sure how much of it actually applies to today's times anyway. Sure, I'll acknowledge those guys, but don't ask me to really talk about them to someone else. After all, I've got to enjoy this life while I can – I'll get around to really worshiping those guys when I'm in the rest home some day. And besides, what will my friends think if I tell them I am serious about my faith in Jesus Christ – they might think I'm a Jesus freak and then I'm out of the 'in' crowd."

If any of these thoughts register with you, you may ask yourself if you really do have a true faith in Jesus Christ – and start looking for ways to improve your relationship with Him. Understand that He does not just want us to acknowledge Him. Jesus wants a relationship with us. Without that ongoing connection, we are unable to do anything that will be lasting for Him or His Kingdom.

You know, He has a job for me and a job for you. Our work and reason for even being is to accomplish what Christ has already prepared beforehand for us to do. Don't leave Him or yourself hangin'.

"Which" name is above all names?

> **Philippians 2:9-11** Therefore also God highly exalted Him, and bestowed on Him the name **which** is above every name, [10] that at the name of Jesus every knee should bow, of those who are in heaven, and on earth, and under the earth, [11] and that every tongue should confess that Jesus Christ is Lord, to the glory of God the Father.

No mistaken identity here. As we read this account from Paul, there is no doubt that Jesus is the name, not Allah, not Mohammed, not Buddha, not Joseph Smith, not mother-nature, not anyone else in all creation. What do you take this to mean? You know, it doesn't really matter, or does it? It is either true or false, right or wrong, fact or fiction.

The situation is: what are you banking your eternal future on? On gods who state you have to be good enough and do enough good "things" to earn your way to heaven, nirvana, utopia, etc. Or on the One God who came to save us from sin, death, and even from ourselves, and gives us a hope and a future that none of us could ever earn or even hope for without His loving mercy and compassion for us as sinners.

And what happens to the other so-called gods who are in heaven, on earth, and under the earth? It seems very plain to me, as I hope it does to you, that they, along with all the other non-believers will be doing the same thing we believers will be doing at the last Day – bowed on all our knees with our faces to the ground, confessing Jesus Christ is Lord, to the glory of the Father.

The problem is, after that, those non-gods and unbelievers will have an eternal destiny that they will not be happy with - and they won't be happy with it forever!

So, I would ask you to remember: "Which" involves a choice, and "which" ever way we choose will impact where we each spend eternity.

CHAPTER 2 - WAY

To the world there seems to be many "ways!"

> **Jude 1:11** Woe to them! For they have gone the way of Cain, and for pay they have rushed headlong into the error of Balaam, and perished in the rebellion of Korah.

"Mark, there are many roads to the mountain top and the ministers I have for patients have told me there are many ways to heaven. I agree with them and besides, there are many churches in my community and none of them seem to get along very well together. That's the reason I don't go to any church; why would I want to associate myself with people like that? I am finding my own way and road to the top of the mountain, and I am happy with the path I am on. By the way, thanks for trying to help me, but – no thanks!" This was the gist of the email I received from a dentist I had just met in Chicago the previous week.

We had met through a mutual friend and the three of

us walked along the "million-dollar-mile" in Chicago after attending a dental meeting there. During the conversation, I asked my "usual" question to Ron Presswood, my longtime friend and mentor: "Why are we here?" (By the way, you may hear this question numerous times in this book as this is "my question" for life.)

Ron chuckled because he has heard me ask the question so often, he knows it is going to come up each and every time we get together. The other dentist's head kind of "tilted" as he seriously asked, "What's the answer to that question?" I responded I would send him an email of a PowerPoint presentation I had that I felt gave some perspective on what the answer to that question might be. The presentation points to Jesus Christ, His redeeming love and sacrifice, and how He is the answer to the question.

Proverbs 16:25 There is a way *which seems* **right to a man, But its end is the way of death.**

ᴄᴚᴏ

I think a lot of people are misled into seeking a way which "seems" right to them and I believe Satan is a formidable foe who is an expert in deception. Many are fooled into a panoply of reasoning and rationalizations about where they will spend eternity. Part of the problem is that the decisions they are making are having eternal consequences, and much of the time, they may be "choosing" eternal damnation without even realizing it. They don't know that they don't know what the real truth is and frankly, many don't seem to be that concerned about where they will even spend eternity.

That's the sad part, isn't it? Many are seeking a "way" which is obviously the way of the world and unfortunately, it is the "prevalent way" most are consumed with. Our eyes are set on the wrong god of this world, not the one, true God of the universe.

Many are endeavoring to strive for a life that leads to death and an eternity in hell and don't even know it. How about you? Where are you heading for eternity? Have you even thought about it? Does it concern you at all? Cain sought his own way and showed no reverence for God. Does this sound like you?

Please stay with me here as your feelings and thoughts on this can impact you, yes YOU, for the rest of eternity. Satan's deception runs wide and deep and he is a master of it. The "stock" answer I hear from those who may have a "lukewarm" faith is: "But Mark, I'm a good person, I haven't killed anybody or cheated anyone or been unfaithful to my wife!" <u>Guess what: none of those accomplishments will result in your being in heaven for eternity with Christ and the saints!</u>

You see, Satan wants you to buy into that reasoning because if he can get you to buy into that, he's got you right where he wants you; lost to Christ and with him in hell for FOREVER! And it ain't going to be any cakewalk partying along with the other sinners in that place. At the risk of having you put this book down right now and walk away from it for good, I've got to help you to understand what you are probably in for, for the long haul of eternity in hell.

First, there possibly will be a darkness that will be so very dark, so very black, so very oppressive, that you will long for one little glimmer or ray of light; and it won't be there, ever! **(Matthew 8:12)**

Second, you may hear agonizing and piercing screams, groans and cries from your fellow soul-mates who, maybe along with you, are in constant pain and agony – worse than we can even begin to comprehend – forever! **(Luke 16:23-25)**

Third, you will most likely be out of the presence of our Lord and Savior with no chance of EVER being in His presence again, for eternity! **(Luke 13:23-28)**

Fourth, you will have no hope. Despair and anguish will consume you in your lonely state as you are tormented and racked with sorrow over the sins you are being judged for. **(Luke 16:23-31)**

Fifth and certainly not the least, but one of the most sorrowful, the thoughts you will be consumed with are that you had the opportunity to escape all this wretched wrath, but your pride resulted in your rejection of the only One who could have saved you – Jesus Christ! **(Proverbs 16:18)**

> **2 Peter 2:15** forsaking the right **way** they have gone astray, having followed the **way** of Balaam, the *son* of Beor, who loved the wages of unrighteousness,
> ༈

Much more could be said about this terrible place, but

we're looking for the WAY UP. Suffice it to say – none of us would "willingly" choose to spend eternity in hell, but the Scriptures tell us that many will end up there, from a lack of choice and responsibility. There will be many who forsake the right "way", choosing instead, the "way" of the world, which ends in death and condemnation.

> **Jude 1:7** Just as Sodom and Gomorrah and the cities around them, since they in the same **way** as these indulged in gross immorality and went after strange flesh, are exhibited as an example, in undergoing the punishment of eternal fire.
> ༄

How about it? Do you see gross immorality going on in our society and world today? I sure do and guess what? Sometimes I'm in on it when you get right down to it. Even thinking improper thoughts are as bad as the actions themselves Jesus tells us in **Matthew 5**. None of us, not even one, can control our thoughts well enough to be sinless before Him. I have to admit, as I bet you would too, that the world around us seems so very "topsy-turvy," that what is right is wrong and what is wrong is right – it really seems (please excuse the expression) "the world is going to hell in a hand-basket!"

The family, as a principle unit and building-block in God's plan for mankind, has been decimated, broken-down, and ravaged to a point that it is becoming more and more non-existent in our world. People of differing backgrounds and faiths have set their minds on what constitutes a "family" – and many times what one person says it should be composed of is diametrically opposed to what the next one says. Place on top of that the various "agendas" many people have out there in our society and ...... well, you get the picture. And to top it off, if you don't agree with any part of what those in these camps feel are "their rights," you're labeled "intolerant" or a "bigot!" You're not a "progressive thinker," which to me means I'm not "liberal" enough for those who seem very "intolerant" of my opinion of what is right, much less what the Bible says is right. Some have even stated that they would actually consider us, as Christians, "right wing terrorists!"

The Lord provides us each a "way!"

> **Proverbs 4:11** I have directed you in the **way** of wisdom; I have led you in upright paths.

The Lord has provided a "way" of wisdom for us. He does attempt to lead us in upright paths He would love to see us take, for His glory and His honor. Trouble is, we're too busy looking for "our way" to have time to get any direction from Him. And you know, He is so very loving **(1 John 3:16)** so very patient, so very compassionate, that He is not going to force Himself on anyone. Jesus "knocks" at the door of our hearts, He doesn't "break it down!" Well, maybe sometimes – as He did with Paul on the road to Damascus.

1 Corinthians 12:31 But earnestly desire the greater gifts. And I show you a still more excellent **way.**

∞

We have a tendency to earnestly desire the lesser gifts, the worldly treasures we can see and feel and touch. The prestigious accolades we can garner from those in our little corner of this world. We can't see or even conceive of the greater gifts, for they are in a foreign world, a different world that doesn't carry much weight in this transitional and temporary state we find ourselves living in.

Why is this so? Again, "Why Are We Here?" If amassing money, toys, and prideful accomplishments is what we are earnestly after, we have launched our ships on a path that takes us over the falls and into the pit, not the path that leads to the pinnacle of all places possible to be.

The greater gifts are the ones of the Spirit – love, joy, peace, patience, kindness, goodness, faithfulness, humility, and self-control **(Gal. 5:22-23)**. These are the gifts we should be seeking as the Bible so clearly instructs us.

2 Peter 1:5-11 Now for this very reason also, applying all diligence, in your faith supply moral excellence, and in *your* moral excellence, knowledge; ⁶ and in *your* knowledge, self-control, and in *your* self-control, perseverance, and in *your* perseverance, godliness; ⁷ and in *your* godliness, brotherly kindness, and in *your* brotherly kindness, love. ⁸ For if these *qualities* are yours and are increasing, they render you neither useless nor unfruitful in the true knowledge of our Lord Jesus Christ. [9] For he who lacks these *qualities* is blind *or* short-sighted, having forgotten *his* purification from his former sins. [10] Therefore, brethren, be all the more diligent to make certain about His calling and choosing you; for as long as you practice these things, you will never stumble; [11] for in this **way** the entrance into the eternal kingdom of our Lord and Savior Jesus Christ will be abundantly supplied to you.

෬෮

If we applied as much diligence to our faith as we do to our retirement plans, blackberry's, and televisions we would be a lot better off – and so would our world around us. Too often, being a "Christian" only means going to church at Christmas and Easter and saying your family prayer at dinner – maybe. Why is this so? Is it because we have bought in "hook, line, and sinker" to Satan's tremendous deception that we can simply mouth the words, sign a card, pray a prayer and come to the other side of these saying "That's it, I'm in the pearly gates, I'm in like Flint to the Master's side."

Don't be fooled; no, we can't work our way into heaven, but we can't fake our way in either! Do you think for one second that you can fool the God of the universe and "pull one over" on Him? Don't kid yourself, "God will not be mocked", by you or anyone else for that matter **(Gal. 6:7)**.

We ought to be down on our knees often and with all

sincerity, humility, and reverence before our omnipotent Creator each and every day, seeking His face, searching His Word, diligently pursuing a close, intimate relationship with Him. Why do we not do this? We're too busy, too exhausted, too focused on ourselves to want to take time away from us and give the proper time to Him. We don't examine ourselves because we know we won't like what we see **(2 Cor. 13:5)**. So how about you? What do you see when you look in the mirror that reveals what your faith really looks like to the One True God of the universe?

"Way" there is only ONE "WAY!"

> **John 14:6** Jesus said to him, "I am the **way**, and the truth, and the life; no one comes to the Father, but through Me.
>
> ∽✕∽

There is only one "Way" the "true Way", the absolutely positive "Way" the Lord Himself tells us about. The problem for most of us is that it doesn't seem to make logical sense that Jesus could make such a presumptuous claim of absolute deity. He couldn't have really meant what He said, could He? After all, if what He said was true, there sure seems to be a lot of people in the world who are on the wrong path, aren't there? YES, there are! They're worshiping Allah, Muhammad, Buddha, Mother Nature, Self, Humanism – false gods all, who deceive and are massive "stumbling blocks" to the One, True, God of the Universe!

There are a lot of people who are being deceived by the

"ruler of this world" and won't know it until it is too late.

> **Matthew 7:13-14** "Enter by the narrow gate; for the gate is wide, and the **way** is broad that leads to destruction, and **_many_** are those who enter by it. [14] "For the gate is small, and the **way** is narrow that leads to life, and **_few_** are those who find it.
>
> ☜☞

Yes, it is a sad fact; many will not make it to heaven to be with the Lord and His saints for eternity. The "way" is wide and broad that leads to the destruction of many. The "Way" He wants us to seek is the narrow way and how many find it? It certainly doesn't sound like the majority - does it? The last time I looked up the definition of "few"; well, it definitely wasn't the majority.

In fact, in the Words of Jesus very closely after these He says this:

> **Matthew 7:20-23** [20] "So then, you will know them by their fruits. [21] "Not everyone who says to Me, 'Lord, Lord,' will enter the kingdom of heaven; but he who does the will of My Father who is in heaven. [22] "**_Many_** will say to Me on that day, 'Lord, Lord, did we not prophesy in Your name, and in Your name cast out demons, and in Your name perform many miracles?' [23] "And then I will declare to them, "I never knew you; depart from Me, you who practice lawlessness.' "
>
> ☜☞

Now, in these verses, He uses the word "many," so let us get this straight. There are "few" who find the narrow road and "many" who Jesus will tell to depart from Him for He never knew them.

It sounds like there are a lot of people who thought they knew Jesus, but it turns out He didn't know them. He had never had a relationship with them because they had refused Him. They thought they had a relationship with Him, but thinking and doing are two different things altogether. Oh, He had stood there at the door of their hearts, asking them for entrance, actually "knocking" at that door of their hearts, but they would have no part of Him.

Before you say "that's not fair", think about it, here is God the Father making a "Way" for us sinners to be reconciled to Him, and how is the only "Way" He can do it? He asks His only Son, Jesus Christ, to condescend from His lofty position on high along His side, to come to this putrid place, live a life totally obedient to His Father in heaven, let those He came to save mock Him, spit on Him, beat Him to a pulp, whip Him to within an inch of the loveliest human life ever lived, hang Him on a cross to die one of the most despicable and cruel deaths known to man at that time, in order to substitute His perfect sinless life for our totally corrupt, unrighteous, sinful lives.

He did this in order to redeem us to Himself! Now, what's so fair about that? He is absolutely fair, He is absolutely just, He is absolutely true - we are the ones who are none of those, this side of heaven.

WHICH WAY IS UP?

According to Jesus there is only one "Way" – the right "Way", the true "Way." You might say, "Hey Mark, I don't buy it! I don't think Jesus means it the way He says it or the way you say it either." That's fine and that's your prerogative. But I'm putting my faith and betting my future on the One Who says He is the One and only "Way" to the Father, not on my own ability to get there. I put my faith in Him and Him alone! How about you? Still don't buy it?

If you do take that position and stance, get ready, because the dancin' shoes you'll be wearing, if you're wearing any at all, will be on your feet for a long, long time; in fact, for an eternity of bliss or an eternity of torment. And it won't be me who determines where you go either. That's between you and Him.

CHAPTER 3 - IS

"Is" is relevant!

The meaning of the word "is" was recently brought into question. After all, do we really know what the meaning of the word "is" is? "Relativism", "tolerance", "progressive thinking" – all terms we are bombarded with in our "new age" of "progressive" thinkers. Why is it that what used to be "normal" and "accepted" is now no longer proper and progressive in our culture today?

Definitions of terms and words are questioned and discarded to the "recycle bin" of our society as we deem necessary when they don't meet the needs of our "agendas." There's a "whole lotta shakin" going on around us in this world of ours, and a lot of it isn't the good kind of shakin' either.

It all feels as though Satan is getting the upper hand doesn't it? (The corporate "kingpins" are taking shareholders to the cleaners and letting them be stuck with the cleaning bill as well. Enron's greed didn't come from only a few men's greed, it came from many other's greed as well.) What am I trying to get across here? Our world, as well as we individuals, are consumed with who? We are consumed with OURSELVES! Get a load of what Paul writes to Timothy in his second letter - *2 Timothy 3:2-5* *² People will be lovers of themselves, lovers of money, boastful, proud, abusive, disobedient to their parents, ungrateful, unholy, ³ without love, unforgiving, slanderous, without self-control, brutal, not lovers of the good, ⁴ treacherous, rash, conceited, lovers of pleasure rather than lovers of God-- ⁵ having a form of godliness but denying its power.* Unfortunately, there are a lot of so called "Christians" who fit in with this description as well. Why is this?

Because we are all born with a fallen, sinful human nature which we cannot totally escape this side of heaven. There is only one way to escape and that is through the One Who cannot lie to us, cannot be untrue to us, cannot change on us, and oh yes, cannot leave us to ourselves either. Yes, you guessed it: Jesus Christ is our only hope for truth and salvation from this lost world!

> **Numbers 23:19** God **is** not a man, that He should lie, Nor a son of man, that He should repent; Has He said, and will He not do it? Or has He spoken, and will He not make it good?

I know of one thing we can be thankful for, that God is not like us. God can and does do what He says He will do. He answers to no one. I was on the back porch of a couple of my friends/patients visiting with them about 15 years ago. The conversation was the usual stuff: "How's your daughter?" "Fine." "How's your son?" "Fine." and so forth.

I asked if they were attending a church – great question if you want to "cut to the chase" with people. I got a usual answer, "weekends are our relaxing time, we work so hard during the week, you know. Gotta catch up on our sleep." Well the conversation progressed to a point of our talking about faith and God and the wife said, "I'll tell you one thing, if God were sitting right there I'd tell him a thing or two! I'd tell him to take care of all those orphans over in Romania who are not being taken care of!"

It boggles my mind! It really does, to hear people speak of the God of the universe as if He were under their tutelage and instruction! The audacity and irreverence people show to the one and only true God of us all amazes me! I listened to her go on and on about how could God let the unjustness of this world keep going on and why wasn't He doing something about this and about that – if He truly were God!

My wife tells me that sometimes I have the tact of a ball-peen hammer and I guess this time was no exception. I waited for her to finally have to catch a breath from her diatribe and calmly said, "You know, Sue, if God were sitting right there, you'd actually have your nose and face pressed so hard to that concrete in awe of the living God that you wouldn't dare have any suggestions to make to Him. In fact you'd be dead before you could do so." Well, so much for being a "stepping stone", let's just "beat 'em to a pulp" for Christ, right?

I do wish we could get past our worldly eyes and see God for Who He really is – a loving Father Who cares so much

for us that He would do anything that was for our good –
really for our good – if we would only come to Him with
reverential awe and thankfulness. But nooooo! We've got to
tell Him where He's dropping the ball and not performing up
to "our standards."

I think that is a lot of our problem in the here and now.
We are looking at God through our skewed vision of reality,
which is even more skewed than we can imagine. This means
we are trying to tell our Creator that we know better than
He, what needs to be done! I don't think God is scratching
His head saying, "Boy, I wonder how I'm going to be able
to help those orphans in Romania. Sue, have you got any
suggestions for Me?"

God "is" love!

> **1 John 4:16**   [16] And we have come to
> know and have believed the love which
> God has for us. God **is** love, and the one
> who abides in love abides in God, and
> God abides in him.
> ༜

In Henry Blackaby's study Experiencing God, he makes
this point: "God is love. Your total trust in God's love is
crucial. This has been a powerful influence in my life. I
never look at circumstances without seeing them against the
backdrop of the cross. My relationship with God determines
everything I do." Amen, Dr. Blackaby! If only the rest of us
could look at our lives from this perspective! I try, but the
"self" gets in the way.

God's love for us is so very evident that oftentimes we take it for granted and totally lose sight of it while basking in it. How could He, knowing what a knucklehead sinner I am, choose to condescend and come and rescue me from sin, death, and myself? Not only that, why oh why would He send His only Son to pay the price for my sins, hatred, and pride? There is only one reason – He loves me – yes me, and every other sinner who walks the face of this earth. In case you can't put 2&2 together that means you as well. I'm not taking this rap for everybody, like Jesus did.

This verse in **1 John** makes me wonder how many of us "professing Christians" truly do reciprocate God's love and abide in Him. If indeed we do love Him, I would think we would be more apt to show His love of us to others around us. Are you abiding in love? Are you abiding in Jesus Christ? Is God truly abiding in you? These are the truly meaningful questions in our lives, not "look, I go to church and am a good person." He doesn't want part of us, He wants all of us, lock, stock 'n barrel!

"Abiding," interesting word, isn't it? What do you think that word is telling you to do for Him? Webster's: **abiding** - **a:** to endure without yielding : WITHSTAND **b:** to bear patiently **c:** ENDURING, CONTINUING. This is where I feel a lot of us are missing the boat. We raise the hand, walk the aisle, say the prayer, and sign the card... but then what?

Listen to what Andrew Murray says on the last page of his book titled <u>ABIDE IN CHRIST,</u> which, by the way, was written in the late 1800's: *Once again the question comes:*

"Can a feeble child of dust really dwell in fellowship with the King of Glory?" And again the blessed answer has to be given: to maintain that union is the very work for which Christ has all power in heaven and earth at His disposal. The blessing will be given to him who will trust his Lord for it, who in faith and confident expectation ceases not to yield himself to be wholly one with Him. It was an act of wondrous though simple faith in which the soul yielded at first to the Savior. That faith grows up to clearer insight and faster hold of God's truth that we are one with Him in His glory. In that same wondrous faith, wondrously simple but wondrously mighty, the soul learns to abandon itself entirely to the keeping of Christ's almighty power and the actings of His eternal life. Because it knows that it has the Spirit of God dwelling within to communicate all that Christ is, it no longer looks upon it as a burden or a work, but allows the divine life to have its way, to do its work; its faith is the increasing abandonment of self, the expectation and acceptance of all that the love and the power of the Glorified One can perform. In that faith, unbroken fellowship is maintained and growing conformity realized. As with Moses, the fellowship makes partakers of the glory, and the life begins to shine with a brightness not of this world."

My question to each one of us is: "Are our lives shining with a brightness not of this world?"

B.B. Warfield was the Principal/Chancellor of Princeton University from 1887 to 1921 (34 years). Listen to what he says about our walk of faith –

From BB Warfield's The Inspiration and Authority of the Bible, p. 81: "Dealing with man as an intelligent being, God the Lord has saved him by means of a revelation, by which he has been brought into an ever more and more adequate knowledge of God, and been led ever more and more to do his part in working out his own salvation with fear and trembling as he perceived with ever more and more clearness how God is working it out for him through mighty deeds of grace."

Interesting isn't it? How our "Ivy League" universities, which were founded as Christian seminaries, have over the decades evolved as Institutions of "higher learning" with absolute disdain and malfeasance for the Christian faith.

God "is" not mocked!

> **Galatians 6:7** do not be deceived, God **is** not mocked; for whatever a man sows, this he will also reap.

While Murray tells us what it is like to abide in Christ – the yielded soul, the clearer insight, the holding fast to God's truth, and the indwelling of the Spirit – we as believers have a problem with lying do we not? We are all liars if we are truly honest with ourselves. A large part of our problem is who we lie to. Not only do we lie to those around us and to the one true God of the universe, we lie to ourselves as well!

I had a patient come in who, in the middle of a lengthy appointment, asked me out of the blue, "Mark, are you a lay minister?" I immediately responded with, "Why no, Don, I am not." As I grappled with what he had said, it hit me, so I followed up with, "But if you really do think about it, I guess I would have to say yes. Yes, as a Christian, I think we are all truly lay ministers whether we realize it or not. What made you ask me that?"

I'm sure it hadn't missed his well-trained eye that there are Bibles in my reception room, devotionals by Brownlee and Oswald Chambers out there too, along with crosses and Scriptures framed and hung on the walls. As well, there is a library bookcase in which half or more of the books on the shelves are on the subject of Christian faith.

Don replied with a little uneasiness in his voice, "Oh I dunno, I could just tell that you seem to be a man of God and I was curious."

I went on to tell Don, that yes, I am a Christian and I do feel that part of my duty as being such, is to share my faith with others. By being compassionate and caring, along with making it a point to be a "stepping stone" and not a "stumbling block," I have the opportunity to visit with others about Christ. Doors might open for me to have opportunities to share the gospel of Christ with others who may not be believers.

I told him I regularly attended church and a Bible study, taught a Sunday school class for couples, and was involved in my church. That was it, I went on with my procedure, let that soak in, and waited, not mentioning it again.

An hour later, as he was walking out the door with his wife, he said to me, "Pray for me Doc." Now you don't know me, but those who do know that I can't let something like that comment go by without pursuing it. I don't know why, it's just the way He made me, so I said, "Don, wait a minute, come here." And took him a few steps the other direction into my private office. Once there, I asked him, "Have you seen a doctor and gotten a diagnosis of something that I need to pray about for you?"

"Nah, Doc, I'm a non-believer, you know, an agnostic. I was raised Catholic and attended parochial schools all my school years as well. I've been all over the world and seen a lot of heartache and people with no hope who have tried a lot of religions and are still hurting and I just don't buy it anymore. How can a loving God let all this heartache still take place in the world?"

"That's absolutely why He sent His Son, Don, to save us all from ourselves and the heartache Satan and we create," was my response.

"Mark, a loving God couldn't let all this keep going on with no response to it."

"Don, He's given Satan dominion over this world for a period of time; then He will put him and the rest of the world where they will spend eternity. God is in control, He's just allowing Satan some time to wreak his havoc. Do you have a Bible?"

"Yeah I've got a New Testament Bible at home that someone gave me."

"Let me give you some Scripture references that you can look up that could be of help for you and we can have lunch and visit about this again." (I make up a laminated page of verses to give to people if the opportunity arises – it's in the "Resources" section at the back of this book.)

"Okay Doc, just know that I'm a tough nut to crack."

"Don, it's not my job to crack you, that's the Holy Spirit's job, only He can do that. But know this – I will be praying for you each day." And with that, he thanked me, took the Scripture references from me and left.

Two weeks later, I called him and invited him to lunch and made time to not be rushed so we could really discuss our faith, or lack of it. At the outset, Don reiterated that he was going to be a "tough sell" on this "religion" business. Once again, I reassured him that this was not my job.

After listening to him speaking of all the injustice he has seen in the world and all the different religions he had witnessed and all the hypocrites he had seen taking advantage of people through the years, he then made the statement I have heard more than several times from those who say they have no faith: "Mark, how can a loving God let all these problems happen to so many of the people all over this earth? It's a mess!"

That was my queue by the way, so I stated, "Don, it is a messed up world isn't it? That's because we are all sinners, every one of us, aren't we? I am a Christian; I do place my faith in Jesus Christ because He paid the price that I couldn't pay with a righteousness I can't attain without His shed blood as a sacrifice for my sins. He is my only hope, my only opportunity to be rid of the sin and death that everyone of us on this earth truly deserves when you look at it.

"Don, I am a 'scumbag sinner.' Anything I do on my

own is as 'filthy rags' before the throne of God, save what Christ can do through me. When people think they're God's gift to the world, they are trying to take the place of the one true gift – the most precious gift God could have ever given us, His Son. That's where we humans get in trouble, that's pride, and believe me God has no place in heaven for those who place themselves ahead of Him. Don, each and every one of us is going to spend eternity in one place or another – heaven or hell – and eternity is a long, long time!"

"And that's another thing," he said. "I don't think anyone is going to spend forever in hell; nobody's done anything bad enough to deserve that."

I said, "What about Hitler or Stalin or other villains who have been responsible for the deaths of millions? How long would you think they'd be in hell before God let them out?"

He pondered and said, "Oh, about 5 million years, I think that would be about right."

I replied, "Think about it Don, what is 5 million years in the scope of 'forever?' It's a drop-in-the-bucket! That's why I don't try to think for God. God said there will be some in heaven for eternity and some in hell for eternity, and I just accept that."

"Well that's another thing, do you really think that all the Bible says is true – I mean the miracles, the stories, the guy in the belly of the whale?" he said.

"Don, look at me – are you listening to me?" I said. "YES! Yes, I believe it is all true, all factual, with no errors in it whatsoever! How can I explain Moses and around 2 million people waiting by the Red Sea with Pharaoh trying to close in to take them back to Egypt or kill them. But there's God as a pillar of fire between them and Pharaoh, keeping him away, while He opens up the waters and allows the Israelites to cross over on dry land.

"Don, how do you explain that the ground was dry at the bottom of the sea? Then, how do you explain God letting it close up again and drown Pharaoh and his army as they tried to cross on that same dry land? I can't explain that, I have to have faith that that is what happened and I do – I am convinced that is what happened and that it's not some 'folk tale'."

"Man, faith like that is a gift, Mark!"

"You're right, Don, and that gift of faith is available for you as well. Listen, I don't want to be a stumbling block for you, I want to be a stepping stone. I'm not going to 'hammer' you or try to shame you into saying you have a faith like that. It's like I told you, that's not my job, it's His." I said, pointing upward.

Don didn't make a profession of faith at lunch that day. We did however agree to continue the conversation over lunch when he got back from his vacation in a few weeks.

Please understand me here, this man is searching and might not even know it. But through his statements and with his misconceptions, he's "mocking the God of the universe and he doesn't even know it." He is a kind man, a thoughtful man, who loves his wife dearly and wants to do good to those he comes into contact with – I can tell it. He's like so many other people in this world who are trying to do good and don't understand that all the goodness they can muster is not enough to get them into heaven. And he's not in the minority on this aspect of life in this world either.

Where "is" our heart?

> **Jeremiah 17:9** The heart **is** more deceitful than all else And **is** desperately sick; Who can understand it?
> ෴

Speaking of the views of the world; where do you think the majority of the world would rank theirs and mankind's hearts in general? I believe the overwhelming majority would think that the people of the world have "good, moral, and generous hearts." Not so say the Scriptures, and if we will truly reflect and be honest with ourselves, we will agree that God's Word is right. We have no capacity, in and of ourselves, for good – none! That doesn't jive with what the secular world would have us believe, does it? After all, we're good people, we do good things, don't we?

According to Jeremiah our hearts are "more deceitful than all else and...desperately sick." What is with that assessment? We don't like being told our hearts are deceitful and desperately sick do we? I think Satan is very, very sneaky; very, very cunning; and extremely conniving. He is so effective at helping us to have just enough pride, just enough self-righteousness, just enough arrogance that we end up "living the lie", as I call it.

What is "living the lie" you may ask? Here it is in a nutshell: We, as human beings, are all on a search for meaning in our lives. We want to be somebody, have power, impress people, be rich, have a purpose, gain notoriety and fame, and have our 15 minutes of the world knowing who we are out of all the masses of humanity.

In order to accomplish this, we have to seek ways to stand out to those around us. We put our best foot forward, polish up whatever we feel will paint ourselves in a good light, and take our "wares" out to those around us in order to have them see us as something better than we truly are. We get a compliment here, an acknowledgement there, and even an "atta-boy!" sometimes.

This feels good to us and helps us to feel better about ourselves in a major way. Think about it, how did you feel the last time someone gave you a really nice compliment about something you had done; even more so, when you got the compliment for doing something for someone less fortunate and in a bind. I know your first tendency is to "blow it off" and say, "Not me; that stuff doesn't go to my head."

Yeah, right! And it doesn't go to mine either! Come on, admit it, it makes you feel better about yourself and that you deserved the kudos just delivered. It's a little intoxicating, isn't it? It feels good to bask in the glory of helping someone. In fact, it feels so good I'm going to do that some more so other people can know just what a good person I am.

So we expand our sphere to enable more people to see the good that we do in order to get more kudos and more and more. All the while we are doing this, we know deep down that we have thoughts that are inappropriate and sins that these people giving us the kudos don't know anything about.

But Satan whispers in our ear, "That's okay Mark, you're doing more good than bad, so you are at least to the positive and that makes you a good person overall."

He's subtle isn't he? He doesn't have to convince us that we are perfect; he knows he can't do that. All he has to do is convince us that we are more good than bad and because of that, we are worthy of God's love and deserve to get into heaven - because of our own efforts. We end up being like the proverbial "frog in the simmering pan of water." Hey, this water is nice and warm, it feels good. And before you know it you're cooked!

"Living the lie" enables us to feel the compliments from others give us justification for feeling good enough about ourselves to lie to ourselves about just how rotten we are to the core of our beings. The Scriptures tell us there are many people who will say "Lord Lord!" at the day of judgment, begging Him to let them into heaven, only to find themselves cast out and locked out - forever judged and forever tormented with the realization that they have "lived the lie" and are now going to be paying for it for eternity **(Matt. 7:21-23)**!

What God wants "is" us "sanctified" and "holy!"

> **1 Thessalonians 4:3-5** ³ It is God's will that you should be sanctified: that you should avoid sexual immorality; ⁴ that each of you should learn to control his own body in a way that **is** holy and honorable, ⁵ not in passionate lust like the heathen, who do not know God;

Sanctification is a process, and holiness a destination. Paul understood this well in his self-degrading scathing of himself in Romans chapter 7. I wonder if we do. Do we really think about our life and actions we carry-out as Paul did? In some of the chapters in this book I share stories about other people, what they've said, what they've done. Please understand that I am not condemning them or chastising them either. I am simply using their stories as examples of points I have observed not only from them, but from myself and others as well.

You see, we are all fallen, we are all unholy. My charge and reasoning which I have felt compelled to cover in this book is that we need to take a serious look at ourselves, and that opportunity doesn't avail itself to us without serious effort. When was the last time you delved into the subject of "Okay Mark, how are you doing on this walk of faith you say you are walking?"

At a family Christian camp in Montana a couple of years ago, I had the extraordinary blessing of hearing one of the finest expository preachers I have ever heard. I listened to this man twice a day for five days for about 45 minutes each sermon. He doesn't even know how much he impacted me. After hearing his talks, I bought the CD's of his messages and have listened to them probably 5-6 times through because I feel the messages are so profound. His name is Jerry Wragg, and my hat's off to you, Jerry. You impacted me tremendously during that week – and I thank you for it.

You see, dear reader, Jerry was going over John chapter 15. You know, where Jesus is alluding to the fact that His Father is the gardener, He is the vine and we are the branches. And we, as branches, are to partake in bearing fruit for His Kingdom and His glory.

In one of his talks during the week, Jerry described the way we might talk to ourselves at the end of a particularly good fruit bearing day. We might say to ourselves: "You know, I really did a great job for the Lord today. In fact, I'd give myself a '9' on a scale of '10' today."

All the while, our spouses and those around us would be looking at us saying, "Maybe, just maybe you deserve a '5' from my observation." It's funny how we would score ourselves better than those who observe us, isn't it? It's time for me to share a story about myself with you – and do it so that I can maintain my marriage and my family.

It reminded me of when I was at a retreat with four dentist friends in the 1980's. Mike, Joe, Dan, Bryon, and I had been meeting yearly with Dr. Presswood and Bud Hamm was along to facilitate our meeting that year. In one of the exercises, Bud gave us a personality profile trait evaluation. He then went over the results with us discussing our personality traits with all the participants present. Risky business, so you better know and trust one another well.

When Bud got to my evaluation results he said, "Mark, you have an interesting mix of two dominant traits that I don't see real often together. One is that you test very high on the 'competitive' aspect, and the second is that you also score very high on the 'approval' facet as well."

"Okay," I said, "what does that mean?"

Bud said, "What it means is this: not only do you like to beat the heck out of those you're around, you want them to like you for doing it as well." At that, all four of the other guys there pointed at me laughing and shouting, saying, "THAT'S HIM!"

All this to say, I've got my "baggage" and "shortcomings" just like everyone else, if not more. It's kind of like Keyea tells me, "Mark, people can only take so much of Mark Peters! Then they've got to take a break!" Thank the Lord she hasn't decided to take one from me!

Needless to say I fall woefully short each and every day, and make some of the most "bonehead" blunders you can imagine because I, just like everyone else, am a "work in progress." I'm thankful that God hasn't given up on me yet. He still wants me "sanctified" and still wants me "holy!" Praise God!

The one "is" we want to know about!

Matthew 10:32-33 2 Everyone therefore who shall confess Me before men, I will also confess him before My Father who **is** in heaven. 33 But whoever shall deny Me before men, I will also deny him before My Father who **is** in heaven.

ℳ

Jesus knows how we feel about Him; He knows His sheep. Do we know Him well enough to talk to those around us about Him? Do we feel we can keep Jesus in our back pocket like we do the little stones or crosses we can pick up at the Christian bookstore? Let's get right to the crux of the matter – Are you and I ashamed of Jesus?

Have you ever noticed how people are much more comfortable discussing "God" than they are "Jesus?" How about us? How difficult is it for us to speak of Jesus rather than just talk of God? You might admit that there is a difference in how we feel about saying one over the other. Why is this so?

Once again I have to bring up the "pride" attribute we all innately have within us. We are concerned how those around us will feel about us if we talk to them about Jesus. You see, saying "Jesus" is much more personal and defining than saying "God."

Say "God" and we can possibly not offend or make uncomfortable any number of other religious people. We can discuss our religion and beliefs by going "under the radar" of many of those around us. We can pray to "God" and not get under the skin of the Buddhist, the Hindu, or the Jew. If we bring the name Jesus Christ to the fore, then it becomes uncomfortable and uneasy, because we are acknowledging Jesus as Savior and these other religions don't go for that. We are further defining our beliefs and putting our faith in the Son on the line.

Let us be careful who we acknowledge as our God among EVERYONE, not to be brazen and confrontational, but to be clear of Who we worship and Whose we are. After all, we don't want Jesus to be ashamed of us when we come before Him and His Father. In fact, in the verses following these two, Jesus says He didn't come to bring "peace," but instead a "sword."

You see, Jesus, being God, will involve a choice for everyone. Some will say He is our Savior while others will deny it. There is "light" and there is "darkness" in the world, and Jesus is the "sword" Who divides them.

There "is" judgment!

> **John 3:19** [19] "And this **is** the judgment, that the light **is** come into the world, and men loved the darkness rather than

the light; for their deeds were evil.

◌◦◌

I wish I could have quoted this verse from memory for Don at lunch. It would have been so appropriate, so timely, succinct, and to the point. I bet you have the same thing happen to you, times you wish you could go back and say something else to someone you were visiting with.

Judgment is a topic many of us would just as soon skip altogether. We don't like the thought of being held accountable, especially when that accountability could possibly lead to such dire consequences.

In fact, some would just like to gloss over this topic, bury their heads in the sand, and rationalize - You know, God is a loving God. Surely He wouldn't have anyone be condemned to hell for eternity - just like Don had said. God is very clear in His Word that this will take place. It has to, for He could not be the Truth He is and tolerate sin at His side.

Take a look at verses like; **Genesis 18:25, 1 Samuel 2:10, 1 Chronicles 16:33, Psalms 7:11, 9:8, 50:4&6, 51:4, 68:5, 75:7, 82:8, 96:10-13, Ecclesiastes 3:17, Isaiah 11:3-4, Ezekiel 18:30, Acts 17:30-31, Romans 2:12-16, 2 Timothy 4:6-8, Hebrews 10:30-31, James 4:12, 5:9, 1 Peter 4:3-7.** That's a fairly significant list which tells us we should not "gloss over" and discount the fact that God will judge the earth. And that's not all of the references either!

There's a lot of that discounting of God's judgment going on around the world today, but it is most prevalent in our U. S. of A. No one is accountable, everyone is a victim. "It's not my fault I am an alcoholic, I was born this way." "I can't help it that I beat my wife, my father did the same to my mother." Substitute any abhorrent behavior in the blank and the answer is either "I was born that way." or "The home I grew up in caused me to be this way." or some other something that made you end up how you've ended up.

Flip Wilson summed it all up on his TV show: "The devil made me do it!" That excuse may fly with all the "progressive, tolerant, relativism" folks out there, but try telling that tale to the God of the universe and see what He says. We all grow up in different circumstances and we all have choices we have to make. Like it or not, that's the case. Our choices in most all cases though do not involve or take into account the input of God and His Word, do they?

Suffice it to say – there is a better than likely chance that there is going to be a rude awakening for a lot of people on judgment day, because it is not going to go down the way they thought it would. The problem for those who misjudged this day is that when it comes, all accounts in the Scriptures point to the fact that our decisions have already been made and there are no "take backs" no "second chances," no "...but I thoughts" that will be allowed.

Only the oppressive and agonizing realization that the die is cast and judgment made that those who were misguided missed the opportunity to spend eternity in heaven and are doomed to eternity in hell and torment. I think I'll choose faith in the Only One Who can save me from this eternity in agony and total despair – Jesus Christ. How about you?

Keyea asked me how the book was coming this morning and I said, "Fine, but it's not a feel-good book." I know we don't like having the Truth slap us across the face like a cold wet towel, but better to be "slapped by the Truth" than be deceived by "living the lie" and paying the price for it forever.

Guess what, it really is a feel-good book. If the thoughts or ideas of this book help just one person to receive Christ as their Lord and Savior and avoid the pit of hell for eternity, then I would have to say this is a feel-good book.

For all the "progressive" thinkers out there who may not know what the meaning of "is" is, please understand this: Don't think for one second that your psycho-babble will take the place of God's Holy Word and that He will be fooled by it. If you decide not to heed this warning, let me know how it "is" working for you in your eternal future.

CHAPTER 4 - UP

At the end of the last chapter I commented on telling my wife this was not a feel-good book. Well this chapter starts telling the good news which changes the tone of sin and judgment and points to the good news of the resurrected Savior Jesus Christ. That is tremendously good news – the most wondrous and magnificent news any of us could receive! Jesus was and is raised up!

Jesus was and is raised "up!"

> **John 2:19** Jesus answered and said to them, "Destroy this temple, and in three days I will raise it **up**."
> ༄

Yes, this is wonderful news to those who have faith in Him, but silly and unbelievable to those who don't. It was much the same back when Jesus made this statement. You see, He had just driven out the money-changers and those selling sacrifices from the temple who were making a mockery of God's house of worship (sounds like some of our churches today doesn't it?). The Jews weren't real keen on this and asked Him what was up with this bold action.

They said, **(John 2:18) "What sign do You show to us, seeing that You do these things?"** To this, Jesus gave His response and it was not what they were expecting either. He said, **(John 2:19) "Destroy this temple, and in three days I will raise it up."** To the Jews it was laughable – how on God's green earth did this guy, a Nazarene, have the gall to say He could rebuild this temple which took some 46 years to build, in three days? It was impossible and preposterous!

Much the same response of a great number of people today, as well as throughout the ages of mankind's history. We have a problem with trying to understand that we don't have all the answers and that we are not in control as human beings, don't we? It's that old sinful nature thing again. We like to think we have the answers – that we can make sense of whatever comes our way and figure it out.

The thing is, Jesus did it! He and He alone is the One True temple which God sent to us to be our salvation, mediator, and only hope. Jesus did rebuild the temple in three days, the temple that really mattered anyway - Himself!

Acts 1:9-11 And after He had said these things, He was lifted **up** while they were looking on, and a cloud received Him out of their sight. [10] And as they were gazing intently into the sky while He was departing, behold, two men in white clothing stood beside them; [11] and they also said, "Men of Galilee, why do you stand looking into the sky? This Jesus, who has been taken **up** from you into heaven, will come in just the same way as you have watched Him go into heaven."

༯

Jesus Christ's resurrection from the dead, after being killed on a cross, buried in a tomb, and leaving that tomb to sit at the right hand of God the Father in heaven, has no middle ground. It either happened or it didn't. I question whether we people as believers and unbelievers ever really seriously take time to think, really assess and contemplate where we would make a stand one way or the other on this "miracle." We all "talk around the edges" of it, some agreeing, others not, that it is a fact. But if it didn't happen, we Christians are, as Paul said, "of all men most to be pitied" **(1 Cor. 15:19)**.

Acts 2:24 And God raised Him **up** again, putting an end to the agony of death, since it was impossible for Him to be held in its power.

༯

Acts 2:32-33 This Jesus God raised **up** again, to which we are all witnesses. [33] "Therefore having been exalted to the right hand of God, and having received from the Father the promise of the Holy Spirit, He has poured forth this which you both see and hear.

༯

It was not like there were only a few who observed this miracle: there were many witnesses. Jesus appeared to Peter, the twelve disciples, five hundred brethren at one time, James,

and even Paul on the road to Damascus **(1 Cor. 15:5-8)**.
Tell me why on earth all these men would conspire to make
this up and not only risk their standing in their respective
communities, but give up their very lives in various tortuous
deaths because of their absolute surety of the resurrection of
Jesus. They were convinced, convinced beyond the shadow
of doubt, that He was alive again after being assuredly dead,
when taken down from the cross. That is a total conviction
and commitment to His resurrection which I wonder if we
would exhibit if asked to do so.

> **John 17:1** These things Jesus spoke; and
> lifting **up** His eyes to heaven, He said,
> "Father, the hour has come; glorify Thy
> Son, that the Son may glorify Thee."
> 〜

It is a step of faith because we can't figure this one out.
We can't rationalize how it could occur. We can't say,
"Oh yeah! I understand, it makes perfect sense to me!"
The resurrection of Christ is one of the things that sets the
Christian faith so far apart from all others. It is a faith that
requires repentance from our sins, accepting Jesus as our
Lord and Savior, a step of faith, and is freely given – not
a pass into heaven for doing things to earn our own way,
which is at the center of most other religions.

Some Christians may take exception to that last statement:
"It is a faith that requires a step of faith and is freely given."
They may say, "Wait a minute Mark, that sounds like "free
will" theology, what about "election?" I could open up a

whole can of worms here, but that is not the intent of this book, so I will let men much more qualified than I am wrestle with that issue.

By the way, "man's responsibility vs. election" debates have been going on between great theologians for centuries. I sure can't solve that topic. I'll leave the true answer to that dilemma up to the ONLY ONE WHO truly knows how to reconcile them.

So how about you, where do you take a stance? Which do you think – really think – is the case? Is Jesus risen? Or is He not? No one, absolutely no one can answer that question for you, and you will be required to answer one way or another. And the answer you believe in will determine your eternal fate.

Jesus has been given the authority!

> **Isaiah 2:2-4** Now it will come about that In the last days, The mountain of the house of the LORD Will be established as the chief of the mountains, And will be raised above the hills; And all the nations will stream to it. ³ And many peoples will come and say, "Come, let us go **up** to the mountain of the LORD, To the house of the God of Jacob; That He may teach us concerning His ways, And that we may walk in His paths." For the law will go forth from Zion, And the word of the LORD from Jerusalem. ⁴ And He will judge between the nations, And will render decisions for many peoples;

And they will hammer their swords into plowshares, and their spears into pruning hooks. Nation will not lift up sword against nation, And never again will they learn war.

Isaiah 40:31 Yet those who wait for the LORD Will gain new strength; They will mount **up** *with* wings like eagles, They will run and not get tired, They will walk and not become weary.

Matthew 28:18 And Jesus came **up** and spoke to them, saying, "All authority has been given to Me in heaven and on earth."

Not only is Jesus risen, He has been given all authority over the earth as well **(John 17:2, Colossians 1:13-23)**. It is nice to know there is someone in control isn't it? I mean, what if mankind were just left to itself, to do as it pleased. To a certain degree that's what we are seeing right now as our society has, to a large extent, done away with faith in Christ and are "winging it" on their own. With man in control, chaos reigns, and it reigns with a vengeance!

Can you imagine what Jesus is witnessing while anxiously awaiting His Father's command to go and redeem His Church? He looks on as mankind makes exceedingly costly and massive efforts to save an owl, minnow, or mouse habitat – because goodness knows, we wouldn't want to do anything to endanger one of these precious little critters! He stands by as He sees us strive to "save the planet" from the effects of global warming and try to "go green". Jesus must scratch His head as He sees us "grab" for all the wrong things with all the wrong answers and all the wrong priorities. All the while, He watches as millions of unwanted babies are executed, killed, and thrown in the trash can in the name of abortion rights and freedom of choice!

Do we really think He doesn't notice, that He doesn't care, that He won't judge those actions which kill people, oppress them, and grind them into the dust? Listen, Jesus loves us so much that He can't let those atrocities go unpunished; He can't turn His back and ignore all the injustice we commit! Jesus has all authority; it has been given to Him by His Father, and He will exercise that authority to judge the earth as a whole, and each one of us as individuals.

I have a very good friend and spiritual mentor named Russ Massey who says it this way: "Think about this: One day in the future, at some point in time, each one of us will stand in front of God the Father alone – all alone! Imagine it is you because this is going to come to pass whether you believe in Jesus Christ or not. You're standing there in front of God and you are either ecstatic or terrified because you know in your heart of hearts where you stand with Him. Then imagine that He asks you one question: 'Mark, what did you do with My Son during your life?' What is your response going to be?" Will you be ecstatic or terrified?

Jesus raises us "up!"

This world would have none of us contemplate standing in front of God Almighty being asked that question. If we thought of that, it would make us think about "who we are" and "Whose we are" and Satan doesn't want us to think that way. Satan wants us to think and feel that we are self-sufficient and "gods" in and of ourselves. As well, he wants us to feel that we have all the answers.

Funny how that works, isn't it? Kind of ties in with what Jesus said in **Matt 10:39; 16:25; Mark 8:35; Luke 9:24; 17:33; John 6:39**, striving to be self-sufficient and relying on ourselves leads to us "losing our lives." Losing our lives for Him and others is what our lives should really be about. This is the direct opposite of what the world we live in would have us believe: "Go for the gusto!" "Be all that you can be!" "Nice guys finish last!" "If it is to be it is up to me!" "Kill or be killed!" "If it feels good, do it!" – yada, yada, yada.

> **Galatians 2:20** "I have been crucified with Christ; and it is no longer I who live, but Christ lives in me; and the *life* which I now live in the flesh I live by faith in the Son of God, who loved me, and delivered Himself **up** for me.
> ↜

What does it mean to be "crucified with Christ?" Just what it says – we are to be "Christ-centered", not "self-centered." Instead of "going for that gusto" of wasted and worthless idol-worship, we are to give up and lose our lives for Christ and His purposes. Notice how Jesus wasn't out for himself – He always looked for ways to serve those He came into contact with. He became a "servant" as it tells us in **Philippians 2:3-11**.

If you watch Jesus throughout His ministry in the Scriptures, He was always trying to find out where people were in their lives, what problems they were having, and what different needs they had that needed to be addressed. In whatever context they came at Him, whether they were friend or foe, He sought to give them what they truly needed - Himself. Not only that, but He explicitly sought and did His Father's will in addressing their needs as well. In fact, Jesus is still addressing needs to this day; still doing His Father's will today, for each of us who seek Him.

He intercedes for us right now as it says in **Romans 8:27** and **Hebrews 7:24-25**, lifting us along with our needs to the Father. My question for you and me is this: do we even consider that continuously, every moment of every day, our Lord and Savior is raising each one of us who are believers up to His/our Father in prayer, praying for us in ways and for needs we don't even have a clue about? All the while most of us, most of the time, are oblivious and pursuing things not even worth pursuing in the scope of eternity.

Colossians 3:1- 4 If then you have been raised **up** with Christ, keep seeking the things above, where Christ is, seated at the right hand of God. ² Set your mind on the things above, not on the things that are on earth. ³ For you have died and your life is hidden with Christ

in God. ⁴ When Christ, who is our life, is
revealed, then you also will be revealed
with Him in glory.

ᖇᕮᖇ

Christ is where our focus needs to be placed; He is
our Savior as well as our example. He alone can bring us
happiness and contentment which this cold cruel world
cannot deliver no matter how much we like to think it can.

Jesus is at the door knocking and He has his hand
outstretched to take ours if we will but repent, accept it, and
put our goals, desires, and pride away in order to take on
His righteousness. You see, we have no righteousness in and
of ourselves, never have and never will on our own. What
righteousness we have and what goodness we each have done
is as "filthy rags" as explained by a man named Isaiah.

Our sinful human nature is something that will eternally
drag us down until we repent of our sins, receive Jesus Christ
and let Him, the true Servant, into our hearts. Once we do
repent and receive Jesus, it's done; the old is gone and the
new is in place. He clothes us in His righteousness and we
will wear that glorious and exquisite clothing for eternity.
Now that is being "raised up!" This side of heaven we
cannot totally shake that hideous sinful nature, but through
Jesus and His righteousness we can make a dent in the bad
influence it makes on our lives.

Ephesians 2:4-10 But God, being rich
in mercy, because of His great love with
which He loved us, ⁵ even when we
were dead in our transgressions, made

us alive together with Christ (by grace you have been saved), [6] and raised us **up** with Him, and seated us with Him in the heavenly *places*, in Christ Jesus, [7] in order that in the ages to come He might show the surpassing riches of His grace in kindness toward us in Christ Jesus. [8] For by grace you have been saved through faith; and that not of yourselves, *it is* the gift of God; [9] not as a result of works, that no one should boast. [10] For we are His workmanship, created in Christ Jesus for good works, which God prepared beforehand, that we should walk in them.

∽ჟ৹

"...seated us with Him in the heavenly places, in Christ Jesus" – this is hard to wrap our minds around. How can we believe we are to be seated with Christ in the heavenly places? We must believe it because He says it is so. Understand, it is not up to us, and thank God it isn't! We would really mess things up.

This passage in Ephesians plainly tells us we are saved by grace through faith in Jesus. It is very clear that we cannot work our way into heaven. But then it states we are "created in Christ Jesus for good works." We could say this is a paradox or contradiction. It is really not though. We don't work to earn our way into heaven because if we could, we could take credit and have pride in OUR accomplishment. That would be stealing His glory and taking it for ourselves and we could feel "smug" that we are equal to the One who paid the ultimate price to save us. This is not a good thing, nor a true statement.

If we receive Him as our Savior though, we then are dedicating our lives to Him and His will, which in turn, allows us to join in His work while we are here on this earth. Our efforts are then not for ourselves and our own glory, but solely for Jesus Christ, His kingdom, and His glory. Christ alone gets the glory. But we get the gift of being enabled to join in His work and plan, laying those works at the feet of the Lord, looking to Him with a thankful heart that He would allow us to help and assist Him in His plan for the redemption of all the faithful in Him.

What a glorious thought and picture that is. Think of being able to gaze on Jesus, looking into His wondrous eyes full of love for you, and hearing those beautiful words, "Well done good and faithful servant....enter into the joy of your Master." Sign me up for that scenario, wouldn't you agree?

> **1 Corinthians 15:54-55** But when this perishable will have put on the imperishable, and this mortal will have put on immortality, then will come about the saying that is written, "Death is swallowed **up** in victory. [55] O death, where is your victory? O death, where is your sting?"

There are a lot of people in the world who have not even thought of hearing those words from the Master. One inescapable fact that lies right under the surface of all our thoughts and musings for all of our lives is that we are all terminal. Oh, we may gloss over it occasionally, give it some credence in our conversations at a funeral of a friend or loved one; but we try, and try real hard I might add, to not spend too much time thinking about this malady.

We greet each day and put each conversation in the context of "I'm going to live here forever." We set our goals, map out our plans, speak of retirement much like the rich man who filled up his barns with grain in **Luke 12:16-21**. The guy had it made in the shade, had "gone for the gusto" and achieved it, only to die right when he thought he was ready to enjoy the fruits of his labor.

Untimely death has a tendency to jolt us into that reality which lies just under the surface of our cognitive thoughts – that being the reality of our mortality. Not one of us escapes death. Yep, it's a 100%er! Not one of us escapes this little "blip" in the scope of our lives, do we? This is all the more reason to think about where we will spend eternity and how we will get to where we will spend it.

We must be trained "up!"

Cain had a low countenance, he was hacked. Why? Things weren't going **his way** as he saw it. You know the feeling, "Hey Lord, why aren't you blessing me the way I think you should be blessing me? I'm a good person; I haven't killed anybody or anything." Guess what, Cain was getting ready to kill someone, and it was his own brother.

We are depraved, we are sinners, we are unworthy, and

in fact our best efforts toward righteousness are as filthy rags in God's accounting of what is true righteousness, as noted earlier.

That is why we must be trained up as believers. It's a little like boot camp: no training, no results. You see, our walk of faith is not something that happens automatically, it's not as though we can say, "I believe in Jesus." and just go on with our lives carrying that statement with us as some sort of Lotto ticket that gets us into heaven. The God of the universe wants us to grow closer to Him **(James 4:8)**. He wants us to mature in Him and His grace. This is the "process" of "sanctification," of growing and maturing in our faith.

> **Genesis 4:7** "If you do well, will not *your countenance* be lifted **up**? And if you do not do well, sin is crouching at the door; and its desire is for you, but you must master it."
>
> ⌘

Cain's countenance was not lifted up as he was not making his sacrifice to God for the right reasons like Abel was. Cain wasn't giving back to God from a grateful and thankful heart, but from a sense of resentful obligation. At least that is a possible explanation why God was not happy with Cain's sacrifice. Is it possible that Abel took time for his relationship with God, while Cain didn't? I think it is.

Maybe Abel had a caring and sincere heart and cherished his relationship with God the Father, making time to spend time with Him. Maybe Cain resented having to acknowledge that there was a God over him. Possibly, he had so much pride that he found it a real "chore" to even think about spending time with his Creator. Sin was crouching at the door to Cain's heart and ended up mastering him instead of the other way around.

This is a problem we all face in all the decisions we make – sin and Satan desire us. They want to bring us down their dire path because the only hope they have is company in their torment. Satan knows where he is spending eternity and he wants the place full to the brim. Cain bought into Satan's program, how about us?

> **Proverbs 2:6-8** For the LORD gives wisdom; From His mouth *come* knowledge and understanding. [7] He stores **up** sound wisdom for the upright; *He is* a shield to those who walk in integrity, [8] Guarding the paths of justice, And He preserves the way of His godly ones.
> ∽◦∽

We don't have to buy into it though. We can have a thankful and grateful heart, we can have the wisdom which the Lord wants us to have. Our problem is all this doesn't come to us naturally. Sinful human nature comes standard in all of us, it is the one option we can't deny we have on our list of attributes, a kind of a "one size fits all" thing.

So, what to do? Many people, even professing Christians, go through the motions of life without spending time with their Lord in prayer and Bible study on a weekly basis, much less daily. They give "lip service" to our Lord and Savior, but that "lip service" doesn't bring them closer to Him one iota.

Listen dearest reader. You, I, we cannot have a deep, meaningful, heart to heart relationship with Jesus Christ if we do not make any significant effort to do so. Relationships require effort don't they? Certainly they do: no contact, no visiting, no writing, and no conversation for days, weeks, and months on end lead to lost friendships with those we felt we would be the closest to as friends for the rest of our lives.

We all have had it happen – a friend we felt was a "soulmate" whose desires and beliefs were so intertwined with our own that we just knew they would be a big part of our life forever, this side of heaven. Then time went on and "poof." we look around and it hits us, "I wonder what ever happened to so and so, we used to be inseparable. But now, I don't even know where they are! Oh well, it's hard to stay in touch!"

You know what? It is hard to stay in touch, even with those we love dearly, especially in this "hi-tech" world we're living in now. I think all the technology we have at our fingertips actually hinders close relationships with others.

Jesus has sound wisdom for the upright; and He is a shield for those who walk in integrity – but we must have a relationship with Him before He can give us wisdom. Jesus doesn't "sprinkle magic dust" on us when we accept Him as our Lord and say, "Okay, you're sanctified and transformed into My likeness." He wants us to have wisdom and grow in Him and have our minds transformed as stated in **Romans 12:1-2**. He loves us too much to force His way on us though. Being "trained up" takes spending time with Him, developing our relationship with Him, and allowing Him to reveal His will and His ways to us.

A man named A. W. Tozer wrote a book in the 1950's that is a classic called The Pursuit of Man. It is a short little book and a fairly quick read even for a slow reader like me. The second to last chapter in the book is titled "Why the World Cannot Receive." That chapter in this book really resonated with me and led me to come up with a lesson which I have given numerous times to different groups. It goes something like this:

This lesson is the first in a four lesson series the Lord helped me to put together on marriage. At the beginning of the class, I pass out small pieces of paper and ask each person to write down two numbers on it, and then pass them in. No names please!

The top number is "how many minutes (average) per day, for the last seven days, have you spent in "solitudinal, reverential prayer," not driving in the car or before your meals, but 'solely, introspective, personal time' with God the Father in prayer?" To me, it means on my knees, also.

The bottom number is "how many minutes (average) per day, for the last seven days, have you spent 'in His Word'?" They then pass them in.

I then teach the lesson on why many of us don't have a meaningful relationship with Jesus Christ.

I have someone "tally" the two numbers and give us an

"average" amount of time people have spent in "solitudinal prayer" and the number of people who don't spend "any" time in such prayer at all; and likewise, for the time spent in His Word.

I've given this presentation at three different churches, in two different denominations, on five different occasions and the results are usually ...only about 20% actually spend "any" time in this type of prayer with an average time of 5-10 minutes among those who do it at all.

The average number of those who spend "any" time in God's Word each day is about 10% and of those who do, they generally spend only about 5 minutes.

And we wonder why our churches and our faith are in decline!

I share the results with the group, then I share a word picture with them to close the lesson and it goes something like this:

– *We're all "busy," we get up in the morning after hitting the "snooze" button three times...*

...got to get ready...

...got to get the kids going...

...got to read the newspaper...

...got to get make-up on...

...got to get shaved...

...got to get to work on time...

...busy, busy, busy...

...as you're closing the door, rushing out to another harried and hectic day...

...just imagine Jesus is standing on the other side of

the door you're about to close...

...He's got His hands outstretched to you...

...He's looking at you with those eyes full of love for you...

...He's longing to help and comfort you, and He says...

..."Mark, I love you so...I would love to have spent some time with you this morning – helping to comfort you and plan out your busy day...

...although I gave my life for you and you don't have time for me today, please know...

...I will always be here for you...

...when you have the time!

Psalm 119:48 And I shall lift up my hands to Thy commandments, Which I love; And I will meditate on Thy statutes.

It's funny how we have time to spend as much time as we need on "fantasy football" or "farmtown" internet games which have no real redeeming value at all in the scope of eternity, but cannot seem to find any time whatsoever to spend in prayer, Bible study, and relationship with our one true Savior and Lord Jesus Christ, isn't it? Is this "cutting you to the very core" of your faith? I hope so, because we all need to be convicted of a lot of the stuff we do and don't do. Would you not agree?

We will be trained up in whatever we are spending our

time on, whether we want to be or not. Garbage in/garbage out, as they say. I know, I know, "but Mark, I don't have time to spend reading His Word and in prayer!" We all don't have time NOT TO! Hey, we all have the same amount of time, I get no more time than you do. Here's another little word picture to help spur you on to carving out a niche of time for Him – set your alarm 5 minutes earlier than you usually do.

Can you commit to 5 minutes each morning for your Creator, Lord, & Savior? If you can't, you might question whether you've really got a saving faith in Him. Anyway, when the alarm goes off, imagine that it is Jesus Christ Himself nudging you to get up and get out of bed to come spend 5 minutes with Him in prayer.

If you hit the snooze button, just think to yourself, I'm saying "NO!" to the One who paid the price for my sin and saved me from it, eternal damnation, and death. You will want to get up and at least spend some time with Him, thanking Him for your salvation through Him and the price He willingly paid for you. If you will make a commitment to yourself and Jesus that you will do this for a month, you will have formed a habit that will change your life.

I can say this with confidence because I was told about this technique and used it myself and started with 5 minutes a day with Him. Those 5 minutes turned into 10, then 20, then eventually about an hour each morning in prayer and Bible study. I have now been in this mode of spending time with Jesus each morning for some 26 years and I cannot tell you how tremendously it has impacted my life as well as the lives of my family and those around me.

I'm still woefully short of where I need to be on a spiritual basis, but I am such a different person than I would have turned out to be without spending the time with Him each morning. Do you know why? It is because availing myself of Jesus and the indwelling Holy Spirit each morning has brought me closer to Him, closer to His will for my life, and closer to the path He has set out for me, as it says in **Ephesians 2:10 & Romans 7:4**.

Though time I've spent with Him each morning over the last 26 years hasn't changed Jesus one bit, it has changed me! Through it, Jesus has "transformed my mind" to be more in line with His and less with the world's as Paul describes in **Romans 12:1-2**. So, get some training. Just make sure it is the right type of training you are exposing yourself to. We're all going to be trained up in something.

> **Proverbs 22:6** Train **up** a child in the way he should go, Even when he is old he will not depart from it.

We are each devoted to and worship something, whether it is the one true God, false gods, fame, power, sports, gossip, money, or anything there is out there in this wide, wide world. For those of us who are Christians, we are each children of God and we need training. Why is there so much hypocrisy perceived in the Church today? Is it not contributed to by the lack of training up of those within the Church? Many people use church as a social place, a place where they want to get to know some good people, but say, "don't talk to me about the hard questions, I don't want to face them."

Sadly, there are many churches out there which will be more than happy to accommodate them on their wishes. All this is part and parcel to "supervised neglect." <u>We want the reservation in heaven for eternity, but we don't want to pay anything toward the privilege this side of it.</u> We want the relationship, but don't want to devote the time to grow our relationship with Jesus, much less establish a true relationship at all.

So, we give the lip service, we do good things, and we attend a church that tells us what we want to hear, not one that challenges us and spurs us on to true growth in our faith. Thus the term "supervised neglect." We are fooling ourselves and falling into Satan's trap of deception. We "buy into the lie" that we have a relationship with Jesus when we don't. We're going through the motions of "works-based" faith while truly neglecting having a real and vital relationship of an intimate nature with our Lord.

We do this under the guise and tutelage of good leadership within our churches as well as those with poor shepherding. We "go with the masses," thinking we're in by sheer association with the church and group. Not a good thing to hang our hats on really.

We need to realize that our standing with God is solely dependent on His grace and each of our response to that grace. No one can take that stance for us, no one! Yes, Jesus does take a stand for us, interceding to the Father on our behalf, but we each as individuals must make our stand before Him as well. Hence, the training up to even know how to take a stance for Christ.

As I stated earlier, I've been involved in Bible study for some 26 years in some form or fashion, either at church, in small groups, or an organized Bible study. They are all good and helpful, but one study has really stuck out and had the most dramatic impact on my relationship with Christ and that is with a group called Bible Study Fellowship. This non-denominational Bible study brings you four different ways of spending time in His Word – a 40 minute lecture, notes on the passages studied, the answering of questions on an individual basis, and finally, the discussion of those answers in a small group session.

The discipline involved in having specific, daily requirements to accomplish has helped me stay in His Word and devote time to prayer each day. This has had a profound impact on me, my family, and my work through the years. Not that I've not made and don't continue to make many mistakes; but in retrospect, I can tell you that in many ways my mind has been transformed to a better place than it was some 30 years ago.

I might not even have had a family today had it not been for the time spent in this Bible study program. And that is truly not an exaggeration! My wife, two kids, and I have about 60 years of cumulative study in this Bible study organization and I assure you it has been the absolute best thing I could have done to save my marriage, keep it, and have my family being trained up in His Word as well.

Summed "up!"

Romans 13:9 For this, "You shall not commit adultery, You shall not murder, You shall not steal, You shall not covet," and if there is any other commandment, it is summed **up** in this saying, "You shall love your neighbor as yourself."

～✕～

Once again, easy to say, hard to do. How do we as self-centered, self-serving, self-obsessed individuals get out of this "self is god" mentality? We can discuss all the "you shall not's" under the sun, and focus on them all we want, and we will not be able to break our sinful pattern until our minds are transformed to be Christ-centered and other-centered.

My wife and I were proud of our kids as we picked them up at camp one weekend. They had been at Camp Ozark up in Arkansas for their first time ever away from home the previous week. Kailey received the "Order of the Arrow" award for enthusiasm, competitiveness, and good sportsmanship to go along with it. Joseph was awarded the "FIT" award which stands for "first is third," symbolizing being concerned about God first, others second, and ourselves third. A person in doing so, has their priorities straight in dealing with those around them.

You could say that about us in our Christian walk as well, couldn't you? We are to be focused on Christ by spending time in prayer and in His Word each day. By doing so, our minds are changed to be more focused on His perspective than on our own, which enables us to take our minds off our needs and zero in on His needs and the needs of others we come into contact with each day.

This will help us to escape from the "PITS" and start to make the climb to the "PINNACLE" of the sanctified life in Christ He wants us to have. Okay, okay, I know you want to know what these acronyms stand for.

In coming up with a title for a lesson series I was going to teach, I was struck with these acronyms at 2:30 a.m. one morning. I absolutely had to get up and get these down or I would have lost them. Here they are:

"PITS" stands for:
Predisposed Inclination Towards Self
"PINNACLE" stands for:
Personified Intimacy Needed & Nurtured At Christ's Leadership & Example

So where are we in relationship with these? And do we get our own "FIT" award each day? Jesus wants to train us "up", to raise us "up", to be with Him. Are we rebelling against Him? Are we choosing to grovel "down" here on this earth?

CHAPTER 5 - ?

"Mark, answers are cheap, everyone has an answer for everything. What is noteworthy is a good question. Good questions are much more valuable than good answers. Ask good questions and it will take you much farther in life than trying to spew out good answers."

Easy to say, hard to do – as are many things in life. This was a thought posed to me by two of my mentors, Dr. Ron Presswood and Dr. Henry Tanner, both fine men with tremendous integrity. They both modeled "walking the walk and not merely talking the talk." I had already been asking questions, lots of them; but these two men gave me permission that I hadn't really received before from others I had asked questions of. In fact, Henry would give out quarters to those who asked really good questions, but I never saw him give one out for a good answer.

We are all made to "question!"

> **1 Samuel 17:26b & 29** For who is this uncircumcised Philistine, that he should taunt the armies of the living God? ....

But David said, "What have I done now?
Was it not just a **question?**"
∽⌒∾

David asked questions too. You see, he had just come onto the scene at the battlefront to check on his brothers and see what was going on there. It wasn't a pretty picture, there was this really HUGE Philistine taunting the Israelites to no end. And he was doing it quite successfully. All the Israelites were "running scared" from this big thug.

David didn't get it, how could his countrymen let this guy bully them around like this? Who is this guy, "a mere uncircumcised Philistine," to taunt the armies of the living God? After all, the Israelites had God almighty on their side! You know, God plus anyone equals a majority, right?

I think too many of us Christians respond more like David's older brother, Eliab did. We resent those who expose the truth of the power of God to us because it shines a Q-beam spotlight on the paltry, weak, and shallow faith we are exhibiting. Do you ever catch yourself looking at someone who is undergoing such a huge trial in their lives that you know would be absolutely crippling to everyone else who was having the same type problem?

Yet this person has a quiet and rock-solid confidence which can only be explained by the strong faith this person has in Jesus Christ. How do they do that? My wife and I know a couple who are on this unwanted stage at the present time. Kay and Bob have been faithful Christians, raised faithful children, and taught in their church and in Bible studies for years.

For about the last ten of them, Kay has been battling a form of Leukemia which has been chipping away at her life. She has battled courageously, but with a love of the Lord which is so compelling to those who have been on the sidelines watching her slow and painful demise. All the while, Bob has been upbeat, carrying on, and showing his love of her and his thankfulness to the Lord for the many blessings they have received together.

"No" says Bob, "I can't say there aren't some things I would like to see happening differently; but Mark, the Lord is sufficient for each and every day and Kay and I are thankful for each and every one He gives us, no matter what it is." What a statement of faith! I've never heard of anyone who has heard one discouraging word from these two during this entire episode.

Keyea and I visited them at their home one night when Kay was in the last stages of her life this side of heaven. We visited with Bob in the den for a bit – Keyea telling him how much she learned from Kay in her Bible study class, catching up on the kids, and Bob telling us of all the blessings he had been experiencing through this whole ordeal.

The three of us then went into the bedroom where Bob had made sure Kay's hospital bed was set up so she could look out on the beautiful lake out of their bedroom window. As we approached the side of the bed, Kay looked up and gave us a huge smile and her eyes shined with the love of the Lord in them. She spoke as much as her failing strength would let her, we prayed, we cried, and we laughed as she told us to keep Bob from gaining too much weight.

On our way home from the visit, Keyea said, "I couldn't do that, I couldn't be that at peace. I'd be a basket case!" None of us know how we would respond to being in these type circumstances until we are in them. Our prayer needs to be that we can use whatever the situation is to glorify Jesus, ask the right question, and exemplify the love of Christ in all that we do in it – just like Kay and Bob were doing.

I don't know if you have ever heard of David Ring. He is a man of God who has a wonderful testimony and is certainly a great preacher of God's Word in my book. You see, David has cerebral-palsy and has been through the tragic losses of his parents at an early age. I watched him deliver a message on a video a friend had lent me. I think I may have ended up doing the Christian thing and confiscated it from him. Oh well, that's covered in another chapter in the book – Not!

Anyway, back to David Ring. David gives a message on the video about how when we are confronted with difficulties in life, we can go about looking for answers for these trials in two different ways. One question we can ask is, "Why? Why are you letting this happen to me, Lord?" It's a logical question, but one full of self-pity and "wallowing in the mire."

Mr. Ring goes on to tell his story of how he could have focused on this question and really felt sorry for himself for losing his parents while he was still at such a young age with the special needs he had. He shared his feeling of being abandoned by his parents and that God was possibly punishing him for his malady. Yes, people around him would have been very understanding of his taking this approach and feeling this way, but he knew if he did this, it would have done him no good; nor would it have done the Lord or those around him any good either.

No, David, as a teenager, decided to take another approach to his trial. Instead of asking "Why?" he decided to ask "What?" As in "What do you want me to learn from this situation, Lord?" This is such a mature decision made by such a young man. I believe he was 14 years old when his Mother died leaving him with neither parent living.

Wow! To have been so emotionally distraught on losing his Mother, who had been so loving, and nurturing to him; and then be able to turn that around and ask the Lord this type of question is amazing to me. I can only wonder how different our world would be if more people asked this latter question.

Instead, our world and Satan train us up to ask the first question – the "why me?" question. Which of these two are you more likely to ask in your trials? I believe you and I both would do well to seriously consider looking to the "what?" question and not even contemplating the "why?" alternative. Remember, questions are good – but they have to be the right questions.

I asked a "question"!

> Romans 10:17 [17] So, faith *comes* from hearing, and hearing by the word of Christ.

I was teaching down at a dental institute in Miami about 6-7 years ago. We (the dentists taking the course and the instructors) were in the laboratory doing procedures to facilitate excellence in their provisionals (temporary crowns). While the dentists were working on their lab projects at the various lab benches, the teachers were walking around, making themselves available to answer questions and assist the students in any way they needed help with their task.

I was walking behind Steve and had been having some great conversations with him, in which he had impressed me with his sincerity and openness; so I asked him this question.

"So Steve, how's your faith?" It was a vague and fumbled question actually and I wasn't really sure where it came from at the time.

Steve was a little surprised by it because it was out of the blue, but he answered by saying, "Well, it's fine, Mark."

I said, "Great! So where do you go to church?"

"Oh, I really don't go to church – I'm Buddhist."

"Really," I said.

"Yeah, my Dad was one of the leaders of the Buddhist faith in the U.S. So how about you, Mark, what do you believe in?"

"Oh, I believe in Jesus Christ. My wife and I go to church." I responded.

It was just a little dialogue with a couple of questions posed back and forth, and on I went moving around the room to help be available to the other participants. About 45 minutes later, during the same exercise, Steve walked up to me and said, "Mark, why did you ask me that question?"

I replied, "I really don't know."

To which he said, "You know Mark, I don't think it was an accident that you brought that up to me. You see, I have been having some discussions with some others about my faith over the last few weeks and this subject of Christianity has come to the surface in them as well. Would you mind one evening, if we get some time, sitting down with me and telling me about your faith in Jesus Christ and what it means to you? I'd be interested in hearing about it."

"Sure, I would be happy to do that." was my response.

The next morning during my quiet time for Bible study, I looked through my travel Bible (smaller & lighter), which I don't have marked up with a lot of underlining and notes in the margin like my others, and wrote down some verses to go over with Steve one evening. Here's the list along with notes I wrote beside (I keep that small piece of note paper in that Bible to this day – as a reminder):

- 1 John 1:8-9 – we must confess our sins
- Romans 3:20-31 – the "heart" of the gospel
- John 14:6, Acts 4:12, 1 John 5:6-12 – Jesus is the ONLY way
- Romans 8: 37-39 – nothing can separate us
- Ephesians 1:4 – God chose us
- Ephesians 2:8-9 – saved by grace
- 1 Peter 2:24 – Jesus bore our sins
- Matthew 7:21-23 – the scariest verses in the Bible
- Matthew 25:21 – what we long to hear
- 2 Thessalonians 1:3-10 – only Jesus saves us from

destruction
- John 3:35-36 – eternal life vs. God's wrath
- 2 Thessalonians 2:5-12 – some will be deceived
- Romans 1:20 – we are all without excuse
- Colossians 2:8 – don't be deceived

On one of the next nights, Steve and I found some time to sit down and discuss our faith and I went over these Scriptures with him. Steve was very receptive and stated that he had actually been feeling a little convicted by the visits he had had with the other people who had discussed Christ with him earlier. He said that he was going to be thinking about this and the other conversations as well.

When I got back to Conroe, I bought him a Bible, put the tabs in it, taped them on both sides, had his name inscribed on it, underlined & starred the 51 Bible verse references I have made up on a laminated card, taped it on the inside cover, wrote him a note and shipped it to him in California.

When he received it, he called me and thanked me for all my efforts and for taking the time to share my faith with him. That was that and the episode was over, other than the times I remembered to pray for Steve and his possibly reading the Bible and coming to Christ.

That was until about a year later when I received a call from California. Yes, it was Steve on the line. I figured it was a dental question about a procedure, but what I heard from him that day was truly a remarkable and wondrous thing!

Steve said, "Mark, this is the first call I've made and I wanted to let you know that this last weekend, my wife and I both received Jesus Christ as our Lord and Savior." Tears filled my eyes as I listened to his heartfelt thanks and appreciation for my little part played in this decision. You see, it wasn't me, it wasn't those other friends who had pointed him to Jesus, it wasn't the Bible that was sent – it was the Holy Spirit Who had brought Steve and his wife to Christ. I can't help but think that that little five worded question was, however small, a significant piece of the intricate puzzle though.

How many opportunities to ask this little question have passed by me though without my mouthing the words? TOO MANY!

I asked another "question"!

Romans 10:17 [17] **So, faith *comes* from hearing, and hearing by the word of Christ.**

The other day I asked a young lady in her 30's who is a Mother of two, "So Sandra, do you go to church?"

"No, Dr. Peters, I do not go to church. Are you a Christian?"

"Yes I am" I replied.

"You know Dr. Peters, my Aunt in New York is a Christian and she scares me."

"How is that?"

"She is real involved in her church and does many good things for it but, all the while, she doesn't help out her family around her who has needs as well," she said. "It is as though she is so wrapped up in her church and its needs, that she can't see the family members around her who could use some help as well, so I don't know…"

"Do you feel she is a hypocrite, Sandra?" I said.

"Yeah, that's it – she's a hypocrite. She turns her back on her own family, while all her church friends think she is the greatest."

I leaned over and whispered in her ear, "You know, Sandra, if you think about it, we are all hypocrites really. In fact although I'm a Christian, I'm just as big a hypocrite as your Aunt is – maybe bigger. Don't be too hard on your Aunt, she's doing the best she knows how to do; but try not to judge Christianity by how Christians act because they are all people and people will let you down most times. What we really need to do to see what Christianity is supposed to be like is to look to Jesus Christ Himself – He alone is the only example that we can depend on of what a Christian should truly look like."

I asked Sandra to accompany me to my computer case in the other room and got out one of the Four Spiritual Laws tracts I keep in it for these occasions. As I pulled it out I said, "Sandra, all of us are sinners, you, me, and everyone on the face of the planet. And as sinners, when we die, we are going to be judged for our sins." I opened the track and went through the pages which outline the fact that we are all sinners, all separated from God, all destined to be judged for our sins, and that Jesus Christ is the only way to escape that judgment. As I was reading and summarizing the points in the track, I could see the tears starting to roll down her cheeks as she was in rapt attention to what I was showing her. Finally, after going through the four laws, I ask the question, "Would you like to know the only One Who can save you from your sins and the resulting judgment?"

"Yes, yes I would, Dr. Peters," she replied.

Sandra and I prayed the sinners prayer together that day, right there. She was crying, I was crying, and she leaned over and hugged my neck. Her tears of sorrow had turned to tears of joy. It was exciting to watch as she took the laminated Scriptures I gave her and went around seeking out coworkers to show them to and tell them that she had just received Jesus as her Lord and Savior. I guess I've got another Bible I need to put together.

Jesus asked "questions" too!

> **Matthew 22:41-46** [41] Now while the Pharisees were gathered together, Jesus asked them a **question**, [42] saying, **"What do you think about the Christ, whose son is He?"**

Great question, huh? The thing about this question is that one day each of us will have to give an account of what we truly think the answer to this question really is and there is no escaping it. Was Jesus Christ just a good man, was He a prophet, was He a fictional character, or was Jesus the one, true, Son of God the Father?

Jesus asked a similar question in **Matthew 16:13-16** of the disciples. He asks the same question of us as individuals as well. Who do you say He is? Have you really pondered this question and truly considered what is at the core of your heart in regard to your answer? Truth be known, I wonder if many of us ever make the time to genuinely do so. Don't worry, each of us will have to answer it at least once. Each of our answers will impact where we spend eternity, and know this – we won't be able to fake it or fool the one true God. He already knows our true answer before each one of us gives it.

We are at a time when a lot of people around us are asking many questions about where our government is taking us as a country. The government, it seems, is disregarding the law of the land as well as the Constitution of our once great nation. The auto companies are now owned by the UAW, foreign countries, and we tax-payers, who get to fund the huge debt; all the while, the bond-holders got thrown under the bus and were told to "take a hike!" The deadbeat people who have defaulted on the mortgages they attained, which they could not afford, are being buoyed and propped-up by those of us who have followed the rules implemented by our nation for centuries.

In the meantime, our Congress plays the "blame game," claiming they had nothing to do with it while everyone and their dog feels that they actually contributed to and caused this mess. The transparency promised by those in power has been nonexistent and in fact we've had massive debt crammed down our throats and been told to sacrifice and cut back for the good of our country. All the while, we witness massive waste and inept squandering of our hard-earned tax dollars on projects that are so ridiculous we are amazed, to the point of a "grandiose and dazed stupor," that grown men and women can behave in such a manner.

Before you are too judgmental of me for these last comments, please know that I pray for our country, our government, and where our nation as a whole is heading. Believe me – we need it! I actually started this book in February of 2008, in part because of all the patients and friends I had who were so concerned about where our society was going off-course. A year and a half later, it seems we are so much more off a godly course for our nation that it is actually scary.

When our government starts assessing $10,000.00 fines for a minister holding a Bible study in his home, while other organizations are let off scot-free, it gets your attention. While Christians in our nation are not truly persecuted, we can totally say with conviction that our nation is divided by that line in the sand, which is: believers in the one true God verses the secular, humanistic, progressive, transitionalists, who think all believers are just weak, dumb, country folk, "…clinging to their guns and religion."

Yes it's a topsy-turvy world out there right now and we're right in the middle of it. There are a lot of people asking questions. Are they the right ones?

CHAPTER 6 - FROM

We're just "from" dirt!

Hey, get used to it. God is the only One Who is **not** from someone or somewhere. You and me, we're from somewhere and from someone, and we didn't just make ourselves or will ourselves to be born. You and I had no say so as to who we are, when we were born, or to which family we were going to be born into.

> **Genesis 2:7** Then the LORD God formed man of dust **from** the ground, and breathed into his nostrils the breath of life; and man became a living being.

Of course, the evolutionists would have you believe otherwise. It is mind-boggling how much of a stretch it is to buy into the theory of we human beings evolving from some microscopic amoeba which just appeared in a mucky bowl of molecular soup on a planet cascading through space! Where did the amoeba, soup, and planet come from?

Who or what formed it? Oh right, the Big-bang did! Who set-off the Big-bang anyway?

If you haven't watched the movie Expelled by Ben Stein, for heaven's sake, go rent the movie! What an eye-opener, and what a denouncement and indictment of the whole Darwinian Theory! Mr. Stein does a wonderful job exposing the delusional obsession of these so-called brilliant minds. How anyone can look around this remarkably beautiful planet, with the intricate and complex array of environment, plants, animals, oceans, scientific laws, and a universe within the vastness of the edges of the cosmos, and not know there must be a supreme God Who put it all together is beyond me! Tack on top of all that the existence of thinking and feeling people who have such an inner drive to search for meaning, relationships with others, and the God Who formed us, and well… you get the picture.

Why all the "hub-bub" and vehement disagreements about the non-existence of God? One could say, "Well, it is Satan who has misled so many people." And he would be partially, if not wholly, right. On the other hand, I think there is a good case for the old and insidious malady plaguing the universe for most of its long, long time of existence – that being the nemesis of each and every one of us sinners, PRIDE!

Pride is what brought Satan down in the first place, and he uses it to bring us down as well. The evolutionists are bound and determined to not have anyone or anything above them in the order of the cosmos. They instead see themselves as gods. They are the "master of their own destiny." What a pitiful thought to buy into and buy into hook, line, and sinker. These individuals will turn a blind eye to every shred of evidence that there is a Supreme Being or God.

Of course, I guess they would say the same thing about us Christians and how we don't accept the evidences of evolutionary theory. That's where part of the problem lies – their evidence is tainted and manipulated to support their theory and desires. They would try to say the same of the evidence of the existence of Jesus Christ; however, they would lose the argument right there as well. The Scriptures are the most trustworthy writings on the face of this earth.

You don't believe me? Read Josh McDowell's <u>Evidence That Demands a Verdict</u> sometime. He will set your mind spinning with all the trustworthy support of the evidence that the Scriptures are in fact reliable and accurate. I believe Dr. McDowell actually set out to disprove the Scriptures, as well as the resurrection of Christ, and in his attempt to do so, was actually convinced beyond a shadow of doubt that they are indeed the inspired Word of the living God.

You know what is funny about people who set out to disprove the Scriptures? Many of them end up becoming believers in them and the Savior they point to, and in the crucifixion, death, burial, and resurrection of Jesus Christ. You might want to read the writings of C.S. Lewis and Lee Strobel as well; they both set out to do the same thing as Dr. McDowell. They both became Christians also.

Yes, one could argue that these men and all Christians are delusional and lost in their conviction and faith in Jesus. But when we spend time with Him in His Word, He shows us how it really fits together and does make perfect sense in the grand scheme of things. Our God is a God of relationship, love, and sacrifice for all of mankind, so that He and His redeemed people can have a relationship of love for all of eternity.

What is the end in sight for the evolutionists? NOTHING! They didn't come from anything and they aren't going anywhere! If this is what you choose to believe in, so be it; but after having read this chapter, you will have no excuse when you are standing in front of God Almighty one day. You will not be able to say you heard nothing about His Son or His love for you.

God didn't hide Himself "from" us!

> **Genesis 18:17-18** And the LORD said, "Shall I hide **from** Abraham what I am about to do, [18] since Abraham will surely become a great and mighty nation, and in him all the nations of the earth will be blessed?

The fact that God is a God of relationship and love means that He makes Himself available to those He desires to have a relationship with. He is not some great and grand despot, who sits far away, isolated from our world, sending little "zaps" here and there to cajole us into submission. I believe He desires the closest, personal, intimate relationship He can have with us. Unfortunately, we have to remember that relationships go both ways and understand that He has done

His part; we are the ones who have dropped the ball. We don't reciprocate the love for God that He has for us. Why, we ask?

I have a patient named Don who I alluded to in another chapter. His excuse was that he just couldn't believe in a God who let so much heartache and turmoil go on across the globe. He was a retired airline pilot and had flown all over the world for decades, which gave him a lot of opportunities to witness the poor and destitute people in many countries being taken advantage of by corrupt and inhumane governments. "How could there be a God Who could sit back and let all this misery go on and on?" was his question to me.

My answer to him was this: "God doesn't sit back, Don. He loves us so much, He sent His own Son to redeem a fallen and lost world in which He has given a temporary dominion for a set time to Satan. And when that time is up, it is judgment day. You see, God desires those who have a love for Him as well."

He is not into creating a bunch of robots and automatons to grovel at His feet. Therefore, He gives us His love and in doing so, He gives us a choice – a choice to come to Him or a choice to reject Him. Our shortfall is that we are born into sin, just like all mankind minus One, the Son sent to sacrifice Himself to redeem those of us who are fallen.

We truly are "from" a depraved state!

> **Matthew 6:13** And do not lead us into temptation, but deliver us **from** evil. *For*

Thine is the kingdom, and the power,
and the glory, forever. Amen.

This depravity of sin is the starting point for each of us and the place that all of us are "from." We can respond to it in many different ways. We can always reflect and say to ourselves, "Well, I didn't ask to be born!" Or, "It's not my fault, I was born this way!" It is the old "I'm a victim!" mentality so prevalent in our world today.

We can try to "will it away" and be in denial for all of our lives. Reality will slap us in the face at some point however, and we will have to take responsibility for our decisions and choices we've made. Imagine this from an article I just read where the author says, "It calls to mind an old cartoon (maybe in the New Yorker). A new arrival is standing amid the flames of Hell talking to the Devil. 'Looks like I guessed wrong,' is the caption." We don't want to guess wrong, do we?

Matthew 1:21 And she will bear a Son; and you shall call His name Jesus, for it is He who will save His people **from** their sins.

Jesus Christ wants to "deliver us from evil" – but we have to want to be delivered from it as well. How can you explain His taking leave from the side of His Father, coming down to take on mankind's very nature, and hanging on that cross for each and every one of us? You can't, except to say that He loves us so, that He wants not one of us to perish in hell for eternity.

Jesus provides the way and the means to escape the death sentence each of us is destined for at birth. He is the bridge over the chasm of the fiery pit of hell over which we hang by a thread as Jonathan Edwards states in his classic sermon – Sinners in the Hands of an Angry God. Edwards states, *"There is nothing that keeps wicked men, at any moment, out of hell, but the mere pleasure of their God."*

Please don't misunderstand for one moment what I'm saying here – it is imperative that you understand what I am saying! We didn't ask to be born, but we each were. We didn't ask to be born into sin, but we each were. We aren't born "good" and "pure" and "perfect" - then expected to maintain that state as best we can in order to "be a good person" – "good enough" to pass the test of God and earn our way into heaven. I think a lot of people are actually in this boat of reasoning and they will be misled by an ever-deceptive Satan into the gates of hell – thinking all the while they are on the path to heaven. Which leads us into our next topic and Scripture reference:

Where we absolutely don't want to be "from!"

I mentioned these next verses in the "Way" chapter. They should give us pause and stop us in our tracks because there is evidence here that there are those who will be deceived into thinking they are going to heaven, but are clearly not on that path. That's why I am mentioning them again.

Matthew 7:21-23 "Not everyone who says to Me, 'Lord, Lord,' will enter the kingdom of heaven; but he who does the will of My Father who is in heaven. [22] Many will say to Me on that day, 'Lord, Lord, did we not prophesy in Your name, and in Your name cast out demons, and in Your name perform many miracles?' [23] And then I will declare to them, 'I never knew you; depart **from** Me, you who practice lawlessness.' "

By stating that they did things "in His name," these people actually thought they were doing things according to the will of God. Now, couple these verses from Matthew with these next verses from Luke and see if you think Jesus wants us to take note.

Luke 13:23-28 [23] And someone said to Him, "Lord, are there *just* a few who are being saved?" And He said to them, [24] "Strive to enter by the narrow door; for many, I tell you, will seek to enter and will not be able. [25] Once the head of the house gets up and shuts the door, and you begin to stand outside and knock on the door, saying, 'Lord, open up to us!' then He will answer and say to you, 'I do not know where you are from.' [26] Then you will begin to say, 'We ate and drank in Your presence, and You taught in our streets' [27] and He will say, 'I tell you, I do not know where you are from; depart **from** Me, all you evildoers.' [28]

> There will be weeping and gnashing of
> teeth there when you see Abraham and
> Isaac and Jacob and all the prophets
> in the kingdom of God, but yourselves
> being cast out."

To me, these two passages are some of the scariest and most disconcerting verses in the whole Bible. What do you think? Do they scare you? They concern me because it is very obvious that these people all think they are going to heaven. They think they know Jesus Christ. Not only do they think they know Him by pleading with Him by His rightful name, they even start listing all of their accomplishments – works they have done, and done in His name.

Or so they each thought. Can you imagine? Can you really imagine what will be going on in these people's minds as they are standing at the gates of heaven? Here they are, excited beyond their wildest dreams, anticipating heaven for eternity – back slapping and high-fiving one another, jumping up and down, and ready to roll on into eternal bliss. Only to start to feel and hear a quietness and sense a solemn pall coming over the crowd. "What's the deal?" says one.

"Hey, step on in." yells another to the crowd in front. But there is no movement other than a slight pressing of the crowd toward the gate. Finally, there is total silence, the time has come, the first sense that there is a problem is wafting through the air. It's eerie really, they all stand silent, looking to Jesus standing at the gate where He is barring any of them from entering.

One of the many ultimately breaks the deafening

silence with a quiet, weak voice and quivering lips and asks, "Lord, You're blocking our way. Let us in." Jesus stands at the gate, silent and looking out over the massive crowd of stunned people

Another says, "Lord, I prophesied in your name – I even taught Sunday school at my church." Still another says, "Lord, I cast out demons in your name and performed miracles at your behest." It starts to be apparent that these throngs are not going to be admitted and the pressing of the crowd toward the lone gate gets more intense.

Murmuring and shouts start to come out throughout the sea of people – the push to get through the gate is reaching a feverish pitch. Cries of "Lord, Lord!"; "let me in!" "No, me!" "Not them, but me!" It is all downhill from here, figuratively and literally.

Finally, as things are getting out of control, the pushing and shoving, the cries of anguish from the realization they may not be admitted are echoing throughout the ranks of the multitude of people, Jesus raises His hand and silences the crowd. At last! The people seem relieved, "He will let us in now – it was just a misunderstanding." Their hearts start to well up with gratitude and love for the Savior they never really spent time with in their self-centered, busy days while being consumed with the worldly idols around them.

There was a split-second glimmer of hope for the crowd..... to their dismay, that glimmer is dashed to pieces when the Christ, the One True Son of God shouts out over the deafening silence: "Depart from Me, for I never knew you."

It is done. He steps inside the gate, closes it with a loud and terrifying "thud" and then the reality of what has just taken place comes over the people with a swiftness and a certainty which not one of them can deny – each one of them is "DOOMED!" Sentenced to eternal torment and torture for eons and eons, with no hope of ever even getting a "drop" of water to quench the fiery burning of their tongues or even a hope of ever escaping the agonizing pain of the worms which have started eating their wretched flesh – FOREVER!

TAKE A BREATH! BREATHE DEEPLY – EXHALE – AND GATHER YOURSELF!

I had never really envisioned this scenario – and probably wouldn't have were it not for three individuals who I've either read or listened to. They are Jonathan Edwards (Sinners in the Hands of an Angry God), Charles Haddon Spurgeon (The Wailing of Risca), and John MacArthur (Heaven! Narrow or Broad Gate?).

I know this is a topic all of us want to avoid and not even think about, but what if? What if this will be the case for some – or many – as the Scriptures state. Where are you going to be? Within the gate – or without – they are going to be two very different places with two very different outcomes. Which one will you be "from" in the eternal future?

Jesus warns us earlier in the same chapter in Matthew that to get into that gate and be "from" heaven in eternity future will be the exception and not the rule.

Matthew 7:13-14 [3] "Enter by the narrow gate; for the gate is wide, and the way is broad that leads to destruction, and many are those who enter by it. [14] "For the gate is small, and the way is narrow that leads to life, and few are those who find it.

ॐ

There are a lot of people happily going through this life – content to take in the world and all it has to offer and thinking to themselves, "I don't believe in God! Oh I believe we have spirits which never die, but I don't buy into this religion stuff. There are too many hypocrites in churches."

I spoke with a lady in my practice recently, we'll call her Bev. This quote was almost verbatim what Bev expressed to me the other day as we sat visiting about the state of our nation, government, and economy. We were actually having this conversation because she was voicing concern over where our country is headed in these turbulent days. We had gotten to the hypocrite remark because she had asked me what I thought about where things were going.

My comment to her was, "Bev, I don't know where you stand on the issue of having faith in God, but I am a Christian and I want to be certain where my family and I spend eternity. I feel they and I may have to take a stand for our faith during these difficult times – so I am trying to prepare all of us to be able to do that." I could see the tell-tale glaze come over her eyes at the hint of this thought. You may know that look if you've ever tried to visit with a friend about your faith.

She stayed with me though and didn't totally shut me

down. She said her husband had gotten their kids baptized because he wanted to do so. Why she really didn't know. Maybe "to cover their bases," she said. Bev related that she didn't want to force or impose her views and beliefs on her kids. Where do people get this notion? I don't know who or what gets this idea into people's minds, other than some people who want nothing less than a society which has no morals, standards, or faith in anything other than "Mother Earth!" What a sad position to hold onto though.

This lady is one of the nicest and sweetest people you would want to meet. She obviously loves her kids, loves her husband, and wants the very best of everything for their family. I responded, "Yes, I understand that a lot of people take that approach with their kids. But Bev, my wife and I decided that doing that would be leaving it up to this crazy world to train up our kids – and we don't want that to happen." We definitely need to train up our kids.

You could see that this did register with her and give her something to ponder. I then proceeded to help her understand how I used to be in the same camp she is in now, but that my faith in Jesus Christ had changed my viewpoint. I was careful to not be judgmental, not be arrogant, and not be condescending to her. She was searching and she didn't even know it. Isn't that the case with a lot of people? Virtually everyone is searching – and they don't know where to find the answers to what they are doing with their lives.

I told Bev I was writing this book and said to her, "Do you know who it's for?"

She said, "Me?"

I told her, "yes," and you could see her eyes start to glisten with tears. She now knew she was searching and saw something she thought might be of interest and help to her, but she was still resolved to hold off on taking too much of the bait at one time. I sensed that and asked her if she would be offended if I offered her a small short tract (Bill Bright's – Four Spiritual Laws) for her and her husband to read. She took it, we spoke a little more, and I told her I would see her on her next visit.

The wide road or the narrow, the many or the few – which path are you on? Be careful, whichever one you are on will determine where you will be "from" in the eternal future.

CHAPTER 7 - AMONGST

"Amongst" the lost of this world!

Now, this is where it starts to get dicey. We've just been hearing about the wide vs. the narrow road – and the belief that the two roads don't really go to the same place – right? So now we start looking at how we got to this juncture and what can be our response to it – both as Christians and nonbelievers.

I don't know about you, but it seems to me that each and every person I come in contact with has some sort of baggage they are lugging around with them wherever they go. Have you noticed that? Baggage of self-inflicted problems, family problems, anger problems, health problems, I could fill another book right here listing the different problems which encompass those in our society today – I bet you could too. It is as if they are dragging a 50 lb. ball & chain behind themselves.

I'll mention again our main problem, and it is the same one that snagged the devil himself, it is PRIDE. Pride is our enemy, it is our nemesis, and it leads to our downfall, just like it did old Lucifer. Take a look at the next Scripture reference:

Luke 10:18 And He said to them, "I was watching Satan fall from heaven like lightning.

Satan's pride garnered him a fall from heaven and God's grace, which put him in direct enmity with God the Father. Not being content to just have his meltdown and fade away into the sunset, the Devil wants others to be amongst him for eternity; so he deceived Adam and Eve. In doing so, he gained the entire human race as fallen followers of him. He weaves his web of deception throughout this world, gathering the fallen in an attempt to have as many of them to himself as he possibly can.

Luke 8:12 And those beside the road are those who have heard; then the devil comes and takes away the word from their heart, so that they may not believe and be saved.

Satan even looks to take those who have heard the Word of God in order to snatch them away from a saving faith in Christ. So, he's a workin' and a workin' trying to thwart any and all of God's plans for all those who would be saved. He accomplished it with Adam and Eve and he did so with the sons of Israel as well.

> **Judges 2:11-13** Then the sons of Israel did evil in the sight of the LORD, and served the Baals, [12] and they forsook the LORD, the God of their fathers, who had brought them out of the land of Egypt, and followed other gods from *among* the gods of the peoples who were around them, and bowed themselves down to them; thus they provoked the LORD to anger. [13] So they forsook the LORD and served Baal and the Ashtaroth.

Here's the setting: The Lord God Almighty has chosen His people, cared for them, loved them, protected them, and led them to the land which He had promised Abraham to give them. Moses had died just before entering the promised land, so Joshua was in charge of God's people and had brought them into that place they had been so longing. They were directed by God not to worship other gods in the land and to remove the other religions and people so as not to be tempted to worship their false gods.

This does not seem to fit with the "progressive" mindset of our day, so I guess we could surmise that God is "intolerant!" Just like He tells us in His ten commandments – He is a jealous God and He will not tolerate the worship of ANY god but Himself.

Guess what? The people didn't do what God told them – does this sound familiar? After leading the people, Joshua died, along with most of the first generation of those who had crossed the Jordan to occupy the land. They allowed themselves to intermarry with those they were told to remove from the land. As a result, their belief in the God of their fathers was intermingled and sometimes replaced by the worship of the false gods of those who lived in the promised land. We hear of this all the time, even today. Couples fall in love, marry, and discover they have differences of opinions as to which church they should attend, what they should put their faith in, and what to do about where the kids should worship because they are caught in the middle.

It kind of sounds like these people felt that they knew better than God what they should do and that they let their PRIDE and self-centeredness get in the way of God's directions. They, and we, want to be gods of our own lives. Do we do that today? Absolutely! Did Satan do it eons ago? Yes he did!

We do the same thing that Satan and these people new to the promised land did. We forsake the God who brought us here. This is the fallen world we are born into. It is the world and the people that we are amongst for this brief time we have on this earth. Scriptures tell us that God gives Satan his say so and dominion on this earth for a time, but only for a time.

Then at some point, God will say that time is up, and He'll do it in His own timeframe. When that happens, Satan's power over this world will end. So you could say we are living in enemy territory while we are on this earth this side of heaven. But our time here is only a precursor to our eternity somewhere else. I am convinced that will be one of two places, just like the Bible states.

> **Psalm 44:11-14** Thou dost give us as
> sheep to be eaten, And hast scattered
> us **among** the nations. 12 Thou dost
> sell Thy people cheaply, And hast not
> profited by their sale. 13 Thou dost
> make us a reproach to our neighbors, A
> scoffing and a derision to those around
> us. 14 Thou dost make us a byword
> **among** the nations, A laughingstock
> **among** the peoples.

Sometimes it feels as though we are being eaten up by this world, doesn't it? I don't think it matters whether you are a Christian or not, this world will chew you up and spit you out. All of us have felt the cold, hard, and callous rebuke and rebuff of the world we live in.

People, including me, have an aversion to being a laughingstock, and that is a major part of our problem. We want to fit in and be accepted by those around us. We want the invitations to the right parties, the right social events, the gatherings that include the "in crowd." It is that PRIDE thing again and again, isn't it?

We compromise our values and our very souls in order to be a part of what this world calls great. We aren't little isolated islands who keep their distance from everyone. Oh, I know, there are those who are reclusive, but the vast majority of us are social "wannabe's." Some of us even thrive on social interaction.

Put me in a room with a bunch of total strangers and within 5 minutes I'm holding a pretty in-depth conversation with at least a large potted plant in the corner. I engage people, I like to find out who they are and where they are from. What do they do for a living, where did they go to school, where do they go to church?

Wait a minute – "where do they go to church?" Why that's social taboo, isn't it. You don't ask people questions about religion – especially when you're first meeting them. To me, it is an innocuous question and it tells me a lot about the person I am talking to by the way they respond. In fact, I think asking a person that question – "So where do you go to church?" – is one of the best I can ask to find out where that person is coming from and what their outlook on life is.

I have had many different answers to it some of which are:

- "Oh, I go to First so and so and am very blessed to have such a great church home. Where do you attend?"
- "I don't go to church, never have, never will!"
- "I used to go, but it has been a long time since I've been back. I guess I just got out of the habit."
- "All my life up until I was 18, I was dragged to church every Wednesday night and twice on Sundays because my father was a deacon. I've attended church all I'm going to in this lifetime – and it was all back then."
- "Since the kids have gone off to college, we've just let that part of our life kind of drift away. I know we really should be going to a church, but we just can't find one we are comfortable with."
- "We've thought about it, but just haven't gone – we just feel there are a lot of hypocritical people at church."

- "I watch the televangelists on Sunday morning."
- "I don't go to church."

You can tell a lot about where a person is, even a new acquaintance, by their response to this question. Just by looking at these answers, you can tell you have opportunities to follow up with interesting dialogue. I can say this, in the 20-plus years I've been asking people this question, I don't think I could count the fingers, even on one hand, where someone seemed remotely offended by it.

Why do I ask the question? Listen, if we are in enemy territory while on this earth, I want to know whose side people are on, not to attack them, but to help them, to help them to not be deceived by the enemy we believers have on this earth. What better way to be able to help someone than to show interest in them – interest in who they are, what they think, and what is important to them.

If I can find out where they are on their walk of faith or lack of it, then I can encourage them and possibly plant a seed to either help them go further along the path they are already on or take the first step of faith in Jesus Christ. In doing so, if I am a laughingstock to those around me, so be it. I think this is important work we have to do here - important enough to stake my life and reputation along with a little humiliation on it.

> **Psalm 12:1** Help, LORD, for the godly man ceases to be, For the faithful disappear from **among** the sons of men.
>
> ✺

I recently received word that Kay died. She was one of the Teaching Leaders of Keyea's BSF group for about 9 years. I mentioned earlier that Keyea and I had gone to visit her along with her husband Bob. Many, hundreds of people, would say that Kay was a saint. Kay would have said ,"No way!" She impacted many lives during her brief time on this earth and helped many others to go further along their path of faith in Jesus Christ, but now she is here on this earth no more.

Kay is with our Lord and Savior, reveling in the beauty and glory of His presence and thankful, ever so thankful, for His love of her. You know, heaven is going to be better, much better than we can even imagine! Kay was one of the faithful, one of those who truly made an impact for the Kingdom of God. She was chosen by God before the foundations of the earth were even laid as it tells us in **Ephesians 1:4**.

God chose Kay, Kay responded and showed her love of Him by making Jesus Christ the epicenter of her life. She was God-centered and other-centered rather than being self-centered. What an example she was to all of us who knew of her unfailing commitment to the Lord. One thing Kay had said to Keyea when we had gone to see her before she passed away was – "Keyea, love those who can't love you back!"

What if all the Kay's of the world disappeared from earth? What would that be like?

Guess what? It's coming! There will be a day when all the believers on earth will be taken up and raptured to the Lord in the air. They will disappear from the face of this world and with them will go the presence of the Holy Spirit from the world as well. This is not going to be the same place when that happens – not the same place at all!

Just imagine our world with no element of good whatsoever on it. This will be Satan's "hay-day" – his time to shine. Excuse me, his time of great darkness for our world. This is the time when, like he thought he had a victory over Jesus' death on the cross, he once again will think he's in utter control of this earth. It will be very ugly!

Trust me, you don't want to be here to witness this time on earth. This world without the presence of the Holy Spirit, with only the ultimate presence of the evil of Satan to occupy it, will be evil beyond our wildest nightmares! Evil unchecked, with no containment of the presence of the Holy Spirit through the saints, will escalate to levels unimaginable!

> **1 Corinthians 3:18** Let no man deceive himself. If any man **among** you thinks that he is wise in this age, let him become foolish that he may become wise.

Dear reader, don't be one of those who is deceived and "left behind" to face this utter depravity. Look to the only One Who can save you – the Lord Jesus Christ. Call me a fool, I'll take that title because it is true, I am a fool, a fool for Jesus Christ and trusting only in Him for my deliverance. I have to disagree with those who think we are not a Christian nation – We ARE a Christian nation! We've just left our Christian faith by the wayside because we listened to those who rant and rave about separation of Church and State.

We, as believers, accept our utter depravity and being lost, just like we accept God's sovereignty and omnipotence over all there is in existence. It is like Jesus said repeatedly in **Matt 10:39; 16:25; Mark 8:35; Luke 9:24; 17:33 - Mark 8:35** [35] **"For whoever wishes to save his life shall lose it; but whoever loses his life for My sake and the gospel's shall save it."**

It is a paradox isn't it? Those full of pride in their accomplishments and works, who think they are going to merit the favor of the God of the universe, are going to come to the sad realization that they have been deceived. Their deception is not God's fault – He put all the opportunities to come to Him in front of them while they were here in this life. They were "too wise." They wouldn't repent and receive His gift which was freely offered. How about you?

> **1 Timothy 1:15** It is a trustworthy statement, deserving full acceptance, that Christ Jesus came into the world to save sinners, **among** whom I am foremost *of all.*
> ❧

If Paul was the foremost of sinners, where does that leave us? Anyone who has a high opinion of himself needs to read this Scripture. Who would put himself up on a par with Paul? Not me! Paul was not a fool, he knew where he came from, as well as where he was going. He had received his Lord on the road to Damascus and did not look back. Yet he still knew he was a depraved sinner.

How can we see ourselves any differently when looking honestly at ourselves along side of him. But I hear people say if they had the opportunity, they would tell God a thing or two, by golly! Carefully and gently step back, oh thou who is so brazen and bold! You are fortunate He is still holding you by a thread and has not let that thread break as you are dangling over the pit. Therefore you still have time to receive His Son, and if and when you do, you will be aghast that you were so very ignorant and disrespectful as to even think along those lines.

Ephesians 2:3-10 Among them we too all formerly lived in the lusts of our flesh, indulging the desires of the flesh and of the mind, and were by nature children of wrath, even as the rest. [4] But God, being rich in mercy, because of His great love with which He loved us, [5] even when we were dead in our transgressions, made us alive together with Christ (by grace you have been saved), [6] and raised us up with Him, and seated us with Him in the heavenly *places*, in Christ Jesus, [7] in order that in the ages to come He might show the surpassing riches of His grace in kindness toward us in Christ Jesus. [8] For by grace you have been saved through faith; and that not of yourselves, *it is* the gift of God; [9] not as a result of works, that no one should boast. [10] For we are His workmanship, created in Christ Jesus for good works, which God prepared beforehand, that we should walk in them.

A whole book could be written about these eight verses. They sum up our depravity, God's sovereignty, love, grace, and mercy, Christ's sacrifice and propitiation for our sins, as well as the fact that we cannot save ourselves and have nothing to boast about. Oh yeah, they tell us "Why We Are Here" as well!

God has a job for all the saints of the world, just like He had a job for Kay, which she fulfilled by the way. Likewise, He has a job for you and me. Are you and I doing the job He gave us to do amongst the lost of this world or are we turning our backs on Him? We each will give an account to Him one day, imagine what that might be like….

Here you are, there is no one around, not a soul to turn to and ask for help, no place to run, no place to hide, standing in solitude in front of the God of the universe. Your mind is racing a million miles a minute…what do I do?….what do I say?...this is IT, what I say or do will impact where I spend eternity!

Actually it won't, it's done, it is too late to change the outcome. If you haven't known Jesus Christ as your Lord and Savior up to now, you're toast! What if God says to you, "What have you done with My Son in your life?" What would be your answer?

Would you be one of the ones who says, "Well, I was a good person. I didn't kill anybody." Toast again, burnt toast! You see, God can only tolerate perfection, nothing less and none of us are, nor can we be, perfect!

"Well, what's to do then, we're all doomed!" you might say. Not so fast, there is a Way, the only Way, the Way of

Jesus Christ. You see, He took our sin upon Himself on the Cross and paid the price, the entire penalty for each of our sins. We have the responsibility to REPENT of our sins, receive the gift of His loving grace and kindness and put all of our faith in Him as our only hope. There are many, who try to tag Jesus to their resume in order to cover their bases and give mere lip service to their faith. When we are each standing before God however, the true nature of our faith will be totally evident to Him. If we're only trying to fake our way in, again toast.

"Amongst" the saved!

> **Acts 4:12** And there is salvation in no one else; for there is no other name under heaven that has been given **among** men, by which we must be saved.
>
> ⌒ᗡᗢ⌒

Now THIS, THIS is the place we each want to be! It is the ONE place of perfection, the only perfection that can save us from the pit! It saves us perfectly and it saves us eternally. This place is in the bosom of Jesus Christ. Know this as well, Jesus knows His sheep and He will not be tricked by any false sheep either.

> **John 10:26-28** But you do not believe, because you are not of My sheep. 27 My sheep hear My voice, and I know them, and they follow Me; 28 and I give eternal life to them, and they shall

**never perish; and no one shall snatch
them out of My hand.**

Do any of us really think for one second that we can
fool God Almighty? Yeah, tell me how that's workin' for
ya when all is said and done! Once we've received Jesus,
it doesn't mean we will be perfect and sinless from that
moment on. I keep hearing people say, "All churches are
full of hypocrites!" Do we realize they are profoundly right?
We ALL are hypocrites, even though we claim Christ as our
Savior, we still remain sinful hypocrites.

The difference, is that we Christians KNOW that we
are depraved hypocrites and have no claim on our salvation
other than by throwing ourselves at the foot of His Cross and
receiving the mercy that He offers us so freely when we've
placed our faith in Him and Him alone. After we each have
done that, we are to go and share our story with those He
brings across our path, to try to further His Kingdom, for
His glory.

Oh sure, we will mess up and fall prey to our sinful nature
as long as we are this side of heaven. We will let Him, those
around us, and ourselves down at different times throughout
our lives. But we hold to our faith in Christ to enable us to be
brought back up to try, through His righteousness, to act and
be in our lives on this earth what we already are in position
– fellow heirs with Jesus Christ (**Romans 8:16-17 ¹⁶ The
Spirit Himself bears witness with our spirit that we are
children of God, ¹⁷ and if children, heirs also, heirs of
God and fellow heirs with Christ, if indeed we suffer with**

Him in order that we may also be glorified with *Him*).

So there you have it – with Christ or against Him – we will all be one or the other! We will stray, but He is the Guardian of our souls… **1 Peter 2:24-25** [24] **and He Himself bore our sins in His body on the cross, that we might die to sin and live to righteousness; for by His wounds you were healed. [25] For you were continually straying like sheep, but now you have returned to the Shepherd and Guardian of your souls.** Once we've decided for Him – truly decided to give our lives to Him – we are not TOAST, but HEIRS!

> **2 Corinthians 2:15** For we are a fragrance of Christ to God **among** those who are being saved and **among** those who are perishing;

Yes we do live in a fallen world, don't we? Think of it this way: we each have faith in Christ or we each don't. That said, we can surmise we are each heirs or toast! If we have faith in Jesus, our job assignment is to be a fragrance or witness for Christ to those around us. When we are a good fragrance for Jesus, we are edifying or building-up the Lord's kingdom.

Likewise, when we are a foul fragrance, we are tearing-down His kingdom. Not only that, whatever good fragrance we had exercised before in witnessing for Him is torn down and lost when we stink up our witness. In one of my lessons I ask this question of those I'm speaking to: "Are you a builder-upper? or a tearer-downer?"

When you contemplate it, we are one or the other. Think about all the people you know who you once thought were good or great witnesses of their faith in Christ. They don't have to be prominent people, they could be your next door neighbor, who you thought was the greatest husband on earth. In fact, you wanted your husband to be more like him.

Next thing you know, he's left his wife and kids, taken all the money, and shacked-up with some bimbo in an apartment on the other side of town. If this guy went to church, taught Sunday school, or was an ordained minister, he has just joined the "hypocrite hall of fame" and lost his witness and testimony for Christ. It doesn't mean he's not going to heaven, but you have to question whether he is truly a man of faith.

We are to be a fragrance in order to help all those pieces of toast walking around and about us to become heirs, fellow heirs with Christ and with us. My disclaimer runs throughout this book, because of my own sinful nature, I give off some stench at times myself. Be careful how you smell, there's a lot of "stinky" people out there.

Philippians 2:14-16 Do all things without grumbling or disputing; [15] that you may prove yourselves to be blameless and innocent, children of God above reproach in the midst of a crooked and perverse generation, **among** whom you appear as lights in the world, [16] holding fast the word of life, so that in the day of Christ I may have cause to glory because I did not run in vain nor toil in vain.

This is another one of those – easy to say, tough to do – things. Our nature is to grumble and dispute because we are selfish and want our way. And with the stench wafting through the neighborhood, or the home, or at work, it's tough to be blameless and innocent, right? We are in the midst of a crooked and perverse generation – and it ain't gettin' any better as time goes on either. Nope, in fact, the perverseness of our world is just getting ramped up, primed and ready for the last days – which, by the way, no one knows when that will be – other than God the Father – so don't be deceived.

If we are going to be lights in the world, we have to absolutely hold fast to the Word of life. We must stay in the Word of God – it is imperative for us to do so! If we don't, we have virtually no chance of being lights in this world. His Word changes us, molds us, and transforms our minds from "stinkin' thinkin'" to "kingdom thinking!"

When we avail ourselves to His Holy Word on a daily basis, we can't help but be impacted by it. It reveals our sins to us as well as helping us to understand what it means to live our lives for Him. Not reading His instruction book for our lives leaves us on our own, fending for ourselves, and not in the proper frame of mind to be able to do the right thing for the Kingdom. If we're not in His Word on a daily basis, we have to really question whether we truly have faith in Him.

When we are in His Word, we will see that our grumbling and disputing ways will start to change ever so slightly over time until others can see we are acting and responding differently to situations than we used to. That's when we start being lights to those around us for the good of the Kingdom.

I would ask you to think about your testimony of when and how you actually received Jesus Christ as your Lord and Savior. Even if you grew up in a Christian family and can't put your finger on a certain date, you can relate a time where your faith may have been dramatically changed or rejuvenated at some juncture.

It helped me to write my testimony down. This helped me to solidify the event and think of ways I can relate that time to others in order to share my faith and the Gospel with them. This will be a great "tool" for you in your witness as well!

Some will be "amongst" the lost forever!

> **Revelation 6:15-17** And the kings of the earth and the great men and the commanders and the rich and the strong and every slave and free man, hid themselves in the caves and **among** the rocks of the mountains; [16] and they said to the mountains and to the rocks, "Fall on us and hide us from the presence of Him who sits on the throne, and from the wrath of the Lamb; [17] for the great day of their wrath has come; and who is able to stand?"
>
> ⸙

Unfortunately, there will be those who choose darkness over light no matter what anyone around them does to try to bring them to that light. **John 3:16-21** says "Woe is them!" They have such a hardened and leathery heart there is no way to penetrate it. The only time it will be pierced is when it is in shock and dismay that what it thought was such silly nonsense is in fact reality.

And then it will be too late! They will want death to come and take their torment away, but it will not. Death will not come to ease their minds and let them stop feeling the torment. This torment is forever and it is worse, by far, than we can possibly imagine.

Who will be "amongst" Him for eternity?

> **Revelation 21:3** And I heard a loud voice from the throne, saying, "Behold, the tabernacle of God is **among** men, and He shall dwell **among** them, and they shall be His people, and God Himself shall be **among** them,

Who will be with God for eternity? Those He has chosen and those who have responded to His call. It will be a glorious and wonderful realization of what we had all hoped for and we will be so very thankful that our faith in Him has not been in vain. Just as hell will be more terrible than we could possibly imagine, heaven will be astonishing beyond our wildest dreams and thoughts. It is truly the place where the God of the universe will reign and be amongst His saints. Oh, and again, it will be for eternity!

Will you and I be amongst them?

CHAPTER 8 - ALL

There is a school of thought out in the world of religion that is described by the term "Universalism." From what I understand, it teaches that ultimately all of mankind, no matter what their belief in whatever god they choose to believe in, will end up in heaven for eternity. The difference is that some will have a different path to get there, but all in all, each and every path that is out there leads to heaven. Again, be sure and tell me how that's working for you in the eternal future if this is not the case and the Bible is right.

I think this is one of Satan's most deceptive tactics with which he misleads people. It enables man to work things out for his own pride and lets him attempt to worship the god that he wants him to be; not the God Who truly is. Patrick Morley calls these folks "cultural Christians" and trust me, there's a lot of them out there in this world.

You see, this is an easy way to explain away that there are going to be some people who are not in heaven. After all, come on! We don't want to even think that there may be some who are condemned to hell forever! It could even mean that it is a possibility that the one condemned could be ME! The Bible is explicit and to the point on this issue and makes no bones about the fact that this is not the case. In fact, the Bible tells us that each and every one of us is condemned "from the get go!"

"All" are lost!

> **Romans 3:23** for **all** have sinned and
> fall short of the glory of God,
> ∽

It cannot be much clearer than this, can it? Last time I heard the definition of "all", it meant "the whole bunch!" There is not even one of us, save Christ, who has not sinned. Because of this, we are, each and every one of us, required to pay the penalty of our sins by being subjected to the wrath of God against our sin. This judgment is a "must thing" since God cannot be true to His righteousness and the perfection of His holiness while allowing sin to go unpunished.

It simply is not possible for Him to allow the two to cohabitate with Him in heaven. Thus, evil will be judged, wrath will be meted out, and all the evil will be contained and sentenced to hell for eternity, with no possibility for escape! Evil will be separated out and set apart from righteousness - it just must be!

> **Isaiah 64:6** For **all** of us have become
> like one who is unclean, And **all** our
> righteous deeds are like a filthy garment;
> And **all** of us wither like a leaf, And our
> iniquities, like the wind, take us away.
> ∽

"Yes, but I'm a good person, I try to do good – I haven't killed anybody." How many times have you or I heard that one? No matter what we try to do, we are all still withering away like a leaf, blown away by the sin nature we are each born into. Even when we are trying to do good deeds, they are still as filthy rags because they are done and accomplished by sinners, us.

Does this mean we fold up our tent, gather up our toys and go hole up somewhere because it's no use to even try? Absolutely not! Are we sinners, yes. Are we totally depraved? Unequivocally, you bettcha! Can we escape the sentence we are all born into? With the love of Christ we definitely can!

The Scriptures tell us "all" we need to know!

> **2 Timothy 3:16 - 17 All** Scripture is inspired by God and profitable for teaching, for reproof, for correction, for training in righteousness; [17] that the man of God may be adequate, equipped for every good work.

You can believe this or not, it is what it is! Some do, some don't. A lot of people say that the Bible is just a book written by men about a prophet named Jesus. After spending some 26 years on a daily basis reading and studying it, I would have to disagree with a vengeance as to their assessment and description. The more time I spend in His Holy Word, the more absolutely convinced I am that it truly is the Word of God, which He breathed through His Holy Spirit, through the men who wrote down the Words of God.

Now you may "pooh-pooh" this idea and that's okay, that's your right. The fact is, if it is the true Word of God written by men He directed to do so, what you and I believe is irrelevant – it is the true Word of God! We can each disagree with Him as to whether it is true, just as we can tell Him we don't believe He can condemn us to hell. If it is the Word of God and if He is as powerful as the Scriptures say, what we each say and feel is not going to change the true outcome of what His will shall be.

It's kind of like you and me saying to the sun – "You know, I really don't believe you should come up tomorrow Mr. Sun, I'm going to just disavow that you are going to rise in the morning." We can disagree all we want but we are not going to be able to change the fact that the sun is going to rise in the morning. Likewise, we can disagree that the Bible is written by God through men all we want and it won't change a thing about it. The only thing changed is our personal belief.

Romans 3:19-23 Now we know that whatever the Law says, it speaks to those who are under the Law, that every mouth may be closed, and **all** the world may become accountable to God; [20] because by the works of the Law no flesh will be justified in His sight; for through the Law *comes* the knowledge of sin. [21] But now apart from the Law *the* righteousness of God has been manifested, being witnessed by the Law and the Prophets, [22] even *the*

righteousness of God through faith in
Jesus Christ for **all** those who believe;
for there is no distinction [23] for **all** have
sinned and fall short of the glory of
God.

～✕～

Here is our first verse in this chapter along with a few preceding it. They are very clear that we are all accountable to God. Very clear as well that not one of us can earn our salvation in order to be justified in His sight. Verse 20 makes it obvious that by exposing ourselves to the Law, we are given knowledge of our sin.

We are a Christian nation with Christian forefathers who were mostly men of strong faith. Let me ask you a question. How many Bibles do you have in your home right now? (Imagine the music from Jeopardy playing in the background as you are in deep thought on this one.............okay, time's up!) If you have none, I bet you are in the minority of those reading this book.

I would guess, and it would truly be a guess, that in our home right now we probably have somewhere between 10-15 Bibles. I've got three I can reach right now as I write. I would venture a guess that you have several in your home as well. Even if you haven't gone out in the last 25 years and bought yourself a Bible or had one given to you, chances are you have ole Aunt Martha's or Grandpa Ned's Bible on a bookshelf or in a drawer somewhere.

The point is this: Bibles have one thing in common with all other books – they are worthless if never opened. I bet there are Bibles galore in millions of homes across this "Christian" nation, which have not been opened recently ……… or ever! Again, available "time" is the precious commodity missing – along with desire.

This is a lot of the problem we, as Christians, have in progressing in our faith – the fact that we don't read God's instruction book. If we don't spend time in it, we get no transformation of our minds, no exposure of our sins, and no help to guide us in how we can share His Gospel with those we come in contact with each day. We are on our own and not doing a very good job at doing that either.

> **Romans 5:17-18** For if by the transgression of the one, death reigned through the one, much more those who receive the abundance of grace and of the gift of righteousness will reign in life through the One, Jesus Christ. [18] So then as through one transgression there resulted condemnation to **all** men, even so through one act of righteousness there resulted justification of life to **all** men.

Adam and Eve tried to go it on their own, didn't they? Here they were going along, singing a song, and having a wonderful time in the Garden. They had one thing they were not to do and it had been spelled out to them by God Himself – don't eat of that tree! While Satan was engaging them in conversation, they were forgetting the conversation they had had with God.

They were presented with an opportunity to become like God and know the difference between good and evil. "Forget what God has told you!" said the Devil "He just doesn't want you to be able to be like Him!" They took the bait, which led to all of us taking the bait as well.

Dr. Jay Gross, my pastor, gave a timely message on how Jesus responded to temptation that is a total slam-dunk fit with what I'm writing this morning. Funny how stuff like that seems to happen so often, isn't it? He spoke about how Jesus responded to being tempted by Satan in the wilderness in **Matthew 4:1-11**. Satan tried to tempt Jesus three different times to forsake His Father's will and take things into His own hands.

All three times Jesus responded to Satan by quoting Scriptures which refuted the things Satan was asking Him to do. Jesus knew His Scriptures and He knew that Satan was trying to trick Him. And guess what, Jesus NEVER gave into the temptations Satan kept putting in front of Him all His life on this earth either. Why? It was because of His total obedience and focus on His Father's will for His life.

This is why so many of us fall prey to sin so consistently – as **Ephesians 6** says, we don't spend time in His Bible and therefore do not know how to fight off the flaming darts of the enemy. Jay also gave an analogy which I heard from Russ Massey years ago as well. It is one of those priceless items that could be used on the MasterCard commercials. It goes something like this: "There is no way we can keep the birds (of temptation) from flying over our heads, but we can prevent them from building a nest in our hair." The way we prevent them is by spending time preparing ourselves in order to give the proper response to Satan when he throws his temptations at our feet and in our face. If we are prepared, we have the ability, along with the help of the Holy Spirit, to turn and walk away from it. This does not mean the Devil will give up; but if we resist often enough and stay in Jesus' Holy Word enough, we can thwart Satan's flaming arrows more and more through the power of the Holy Spirit.

> **Romans 10:8-13**   8 But what does it say? "The word is near you, in your mouth and in your heart" that is, the word of faith which we are preaching, 9 that if you confess with your mouth Jesus *as* Lord, and believe in your heart that God raised Him from the dead, you shall be saved; 10 for with the heart man believes, resulting in righteousness, and with the mouth he confesses, resulting in salvation. 11 For the Scripture says, "Whoever believes in Him will not be disappointed." 12 For there is no distinction between Jew and Greek; for the same *Lord* is Lord of all, abounding in riches for all who call upon Him; 13 for "Whoever will call upon the name of the LORD will be saved."
>
> ❧

Here is my routine for my morning time spent with Him:

- I am so used to getting up early, it is a rarity that the alarm even has the chance to go off, so I'm up & into the bathroom to floss my teeth. One of the real disadvantages to being a dentist is that we have to do this every day, 'cause guess what – people are going to ask you if floss your own teeth each day.

- I'm then into the kitchen to get the coffee started percolating.

- Once that's started, it's to the den and on my knees with my head buried in the cushions of a chair in prayer. I envision Jesus Christ standing at the back of the chair looking down on me as I pray. Using the pattern of "ACTS" in prayer has been a way for me to show "Adoration" for God the Father, "Confess" my sins to Him, "Thank" Him for the many blessings He bestows on me and my family, and pray in "Supplication" for my family and those who have needs to be prayed for. One thing I have tried to add to this formula is at the end of this "conversation" with God, which has mostly been my prayers for others, I continue to kneel and focus on Jesus, try to be quiet – and "LISTEN" to what He has to share with me this day. I can't tell you how many times someone's name pops into my head, or a certain situation is brought to my mind that needs prayer and attention. As well, I ask Him to help me not miss opportunities to share Him with others I will come into contact with today. The last thing I pray for is that Jesus would share with me what He knows I need to hear in His Word this morning.

- Then it is over to get my mug of coffee and to the recliner to spend time in His Word. For the last 20 years that time has been involved with BSF studies – reading notes, answering questions, and reflecting on His Word each and every morning. Even during the three months that we don't have BSF, the discipline and habit that has been established spending time in His Bible is so engrained in me now that I can't imagine going even a single day without spending time with Him in fellowship. It does happen on rare occasions, but not many.

- From there, it is onto my workout bike or elliptical – which is where I've found the time to read all the Charles Haddon Spurgeon sermons and various other books on faith.

- The whole process takes about an hour to an hour and a half of time, but puts me in a mind frame which is less centered on self and stuff and more centered on Jesus and others.

Now I know this might be a bit overwhelming to some of you reading this, you will probably never get the "flossing" part of this routine in, right? Really, I know it sounds like a huge chunk of time, but remember, I started with 5-10 minutes per day and I have been on this path of carving out time for Him each morning for 26 years. Just think, men like Martin Luther, John Calvin, and John Wesley spent 4-6 hours a day in prayer alone, much less taking into account their time in Bible study. My admonition to you is that you START spending time with Him for 5-10 minutes each morning and "just do it!" as the Nike commercials say. If you do, He will bless that time and probably multiply it for you.

So is His Word near you, in your mouth and in your heart? Have you confessed Jesus as Lord, believing in your heart that God raised Him from the dead? His Word will truly tell us all we need to know about how to worship our Lord and Savior.

Jesus has a plan for "all" of us!

> **Proverbs 3:5-6** Trust in the LORD with **all** your heart, And do not lean on your own understanding. [6] In **all** your ways acknowledge Him, And He will make your paths straight.
>
> ❧

Not only does the Bible tell us how to worship Jesus, it also tells us that He has a plan for us as well. What is our life about? What are we doing with our life? Is there any rhyme or reason which drives us to do what we do each day? Jesus has a plan for each one of our lives. It is our responsibility to seek Him, and through that seeking, find and do His will He has for each of our lives.

Going out and "winging it" leads us into the trap of doing the wrong things, for the wrong reasons, for the wrong people and frankly, missing the mark on what Jesus has for us to do with our time here. "Missing the mark" is another description of sin. If we miss the mark on what He has for us to do with our lives, we risk the possibility of having more "wood, hay, and straw" than "gold, silver, and precious stones" **(1 Cor.3:7-15)**.

> **Jeremiah 29:11-13** "For I know the plans that I have for you," declares the LORD, "plans for welfare and not for calamity to give you a future and a hope. [12] Then you will call upon Me and come and pray to Me, and I will listen to you. [13] And you will seek Me and find Me, when you search for Me with **all** your heart."
>
> ༄

Yes, He has a plan for our lives, and the plan is for our welfare. We need to call upon Him and go to Him in prayer. We however, do not go to Him; we take it upon ourselves to try to figure out and decide what WE want to do. In so doing, we never even give Him a chance to listen to us or to direct us. We don't even give Jesus the courtesy of asking Him for His guidance and advice for the direction of our lives. We are too busy buying things we don't need, with money we don't have, in an effort to impress people we don't even know very well. No wonder there are so many hypocrites in our churches with countless myriads of dysfunctional tendencies which lead to broken down families and broken down people along with them.

> **Romans 8:28** And we know that God causes **all** things to work together for good to those who love God, to

those who are called according to *His* purpose.
༄

Okay, this is going to be a little "hard hitting" (as if none of the rest of this book has been!) and please understand me here, I need to hear this everyday along with every other Christian out there who is really interested in "walking the walk" and not merely "talking the talk" of faith. God does cause all things to work together for good to those who "LOVE" Him. That is the crux of the matter isn't it? Do we really, and I mean really LOVE Jesus? I'm going to ask you right now to take a break, go over and get your Bible and read **John 14:9-26** to yourself.

Now, read it again and let it truly speak to your heart, mind, and soul. Now, I would ask you to go back and pay particular attention to verses 15, 21, and 23. What is the common thread of these three verses? It is that if we truly love Jesus, we will keep His commandments and His Word.

That my friend is where our most glaring disconnect is. It is in keeping His commands and keeping His Word close to our hearts. The reality that we don't spend time with Him in prayer and in His Word makes me question whether we truly love Him or not. We don't make the time to be able to spend it with Him, so how can we possibly know what His commands are, much less how we are to keep them! In fact, Jesus goes on to tell us just that in verse 24, doesn't He? **John 14:24: He who does not love Me does not keep My words;**

Jesus has "all" authority and holds "all" together!

Matthew 28:18-20 And Jesus came up and spoke to them, saying, "**All** authority has been given to Me in heaven and on earth. [19] Go therefore and make disciples of **all** the nations, baptizing them in the name of the Father and the Son and the Holy Spirit, [20] teaching them to observe **all** that I commanded you; and lo, I am with you always, even to the end of the age.

∽⚬∾

How can we go and make disciples, teaching them all that Jesus has commanded us in His Word if we aren't even familiar enough with them to know what those commandments truly are? The fact is that Jesus holds this world and the universe it sits in together in spite of us. He does it because He loves us and wants us to love Him – not wishing that anyone should perish. **2 Peter 3:9 [9] The Lord is not slow about His promise, as some count slowness, but is patient toward you, not wishing for any to perish but for all to come to repentance.** Jesus is holding the entire universe together, giving the people of this world the time to repent and come to Him. When He does let go, it will be a catastrophic time to be here as it says in **2 Peter 3** and **Matthew 24**.

Colossians 1:17-20 And He is before **all** things, and in Him **all** things hold together. [18] He is also head of the body, the church; and He is the beginning, the first-born from the dead; so that He Himself might come to have first place in everything. [19] For it was the *Father's* good pleasure for **all** the fullness to dwell in Him,   [20] and through Him to reconcile **all** things to Himself, having made peace through the blood of His cross; through Him, *I say*, whether things on earth or things in heaven.

～✕～

Not only does Jesus hold all things together, but He reconciles all things to Himself. As we study His Word, it unfolds the perfect unity of God's ultimate will which shall come to pass – no matter what we think or do about it. We are either with Him or against Him – one or the other.

Isaiah 2:2-4 Now it will come about that In the last days, The mountain of the house of the LORD will be established as the chief of the mountains, And will be raised above the hills; And **all** the nations will stream to it.   [3] And many peoples will come and say, "Come, let us go up to the mountain of the LORD, To the house of the God of Jacob; That He may teach us concerning His ways, And that we may walk in His paths." For the law will go forth from Zion, And the word of the LORD from Jerusalem. [4] And He will judge between the nations, And will render decisions for many peoples; And they will hammer their swords into plowshares, and their spears into pruning hooks. Nation will not lift up sword against nation, And never again will they learn war.

～✕～

Imagine this, no more wars and no more striving, just the absolute perfect joy of God's love and truth and justice keeping all peoples content and at peace. Now that's a PLAN!

We will "all" have to give an account!

> **Matthew 25:32-33** And all the nations will be gathered before Him; and He will separate them from one another, as the shepherd separates the sheep from the goats; [33] and He will put the sheep on His right, and the goats on the left.
>
> ∽✎∼

Some may say, "So I'm a goat instead of a sheep, no big deal." You might want to rethink that – IT IS A BIG DEAL! There are numerous places in the Bible which talk about the topic called "eschatology." What's that, you might ask? (**Eschatology** according to Webster's dictionary means - 1: a branch of theology concerned with the final events in the history of the world or of humankind 2: a belief concerning death, the end of the world, or the ultimate destiny of humankind ; *specifically* : any of various Christian doctrines concerning the Second Coming, the resurrection of the dead, or the Last Judgment.)

This verse in **Matthew** is one of those places – along with **Matthew 24**, chapters in **Daniel, Zechariah, Revelation,** and others – which point to end times. Each of these areas of the Bible are congruent with one another and give us a view of events which will occur at those end times.

One event will be the separation of those saved to heaven

for eternity from those who will be lost and condemned to hell for the same. This refutes the Universalism camp's beliefs that everyone is going to heaven right off the bat, and it does so in numerous places in the Scriptures. Yes, all nations will be gathered before Him, but then comes the separation part of the event. Sheep = eternal bliss with God the Father and the saints **vs**. goats = eternal torment with Satan and his minions. Where will you and I be?

> **Titus 1:15-16** To the pure, **all** things are pure; but to those who are defiled and unbelieving, nothing is pure, but both their mind and their conscience are defiled. [16] They profess to know God, but by *their* deeds they deny *Him*, being detestable and disobedient, and worthless for any good deed.

This verse adds to my concern for those who would profess to know God, but in actuality, they are being deceived by Satan and the world. Other verses in other books of the Bible point to these people who are deceived into thinking they are going to heaven as well... some refer to these people as fools. Some of these would be: the last half of **1 Corinthians** – chapter 1, which discusses the foolish who are perishing. **Colossians 2** speaks of "philosophy and empty deception." **2 Thessalonians** alludes to those who do not know God or the gospel and how they will "pay the penalty of eternal destruction, away from the presence of God." **2 Thessalonians 2:9-12** relates that Satan will deceive those who are perishing, and there are many others. One might tend to cling to the "victim" mind set and say, "But it wasn't my fault!" I'm sorry to have to let you in on something we all really don't want to acknowledge: "When we say that, we are lying to ourselves and we know it – deep down." We each make choices and we will be held accountable for those choices as well.

I'm going to have to ask you to read three chapters in your Bible now. I know it is a rather large and time-consuming task – maybe 20 minutes tops. Twenty minutes is not too much to ask for the possibility of saving our souls for eternity is it? Please read the first three chapters of the book of **Romans** in your Bible – please!

The beginning of chapter 1 alludes to Paul's desire to visit Rome, as well as stating the "crux" of Paul's message in the book of **Romans** in verse 17 which is that "The righteous will live by faith." Supposedly this is the verse that hooked Martin Luther when it was brought to his attention.

In the first chapter, in verse 20, we are told that we are each "without excuse" – so there is no victim mentality allowed. Now revisit verses 21-23 which tell us that we became "futile in our speculation", our "hearts are darkened", and we "become fools!" Look at how we exchanged the glory of God for images, birds, and creatures. How many people do you know who worship "mother nature", the whales, the poor "spotted owls", or the baby seals, while they throw human lives out in the trash dumpster as aborted fetuses? They value the earth and the creatures in it more than they value human life. I wonder how many environmentalists have a love of Christ?

A super-star dies, the T.V. is virtually 95% coverage of them, saying what a great and wonderful person they were. We hold our super-stars up as people to be idolized and worshipped. Please! You see, our values and what we hold up as great and worthy of our worship is really topsy-turvy isn't it?

Romans 1:24 relates or tells about the downfall of mankind. It says "God gave them over" to their lusts and sin. Verse 25 says we exchanged the truth of God for a lie, and worship the creature rather than the Creator – how true is this? Verses 26 & 28 point out the same thing, "God gave them over" to more and more depravity! If there is anything good in man, it seems he doesn't know how to find it on his own. When God leaves man to himself, he goes on a downward spiral to a totally depraved state.

Chapter 2 speaks of God's righteous judgment as well as the inadequacy of trying to live up to the laws of the Old Testament. Chapter 3 helps us to understand that God is faithful, but then states that there is no one who is righteous or does good – not even one. What does God tell us in the last part of **Romans 3**? He lets us know that we have forgiveness of our sins through Jesus Christ. We can have righteousness through faith in Christ and this message is the most wonderful news that we could possibly have for our lost souls. Verses 20-31 of **Romans** chapter 3 are called the "Heart of the Gospel" by some.

2 Corinthians 5:9-10 Therefore also we have as our ambition, whether at home

or absent, to be pleasing to Him. [10] For
we must **all** appear before the judgment
seat of Christ, that each one may be
recompensed for his deeds in the body,
according to what he has done, whether
good or bad.

☙

I wonder how this is going to feel to each one of us, as
we await our time before the judgment seat of Christ. What's
interesting about it to me right now is how obvious it is that
we all don't even give it a second thought as we go about
our daily lives. We are oblivious to the idea that someday,
sooner or later, we will be at this place having to answer to
our Maker concerning what we have done with our lives.

My prayer for you and me is that our first thoughts on this
topic are not right when it happens, but that we contemplate
it and "chew on it" daily and, by doing so, are motivated by
Him to have our lives take on a more meaningful purpose for
Christ and His Kingdom. If this happens for us, we will then
stand before our God and though our countenance will be
subservient and deprecating, we will know we have "fought
the good fight" and "run the race" for our Lord. We will
therefore not be ashamed to be before Him, but be thankful
to be there – not scared out of our living minds.

CHAPTER 9 - THIS

One of my mentors I have mentioned earlier in this book is Dr. Ron Presswood. I have to give a lot of credit to this man for helping me to learn at least two things (but there are many more, Ron!) Ron helped me to learn how to THINK. And he helped me to learn that I needed to start READING. I was taking a course at a post-graduate dental institute and Ron was the visiting faculty.

Now get this – I bet I hadn't read more than one or two books in my entire life outside of required reading for school and here I was at about 31 years of age. His lectures struck a chord with me and spurred me on to start reading and spending less time in front of the "boob-tube." Ron is from Houston and he took me under his wing, so to speak. So I started spending quite a bit of time meeting with him and listening to him. I even tape recorded some of his lectures and would listen to them over and over, because I felt they were so forceful and profound.

Ron had a lecture that was so very insightful for me and one of the most compelling aspects of the lecture was the title: "This Ain't No Dress Rehearsal Baby!" In it, he discussed how we only get one shot and one opportunity to live this life and we don't get any "do-overs." This thought helped me to get a move on trying to find out "Why we are here" in this life and thinking about my own purpose in it.

1 Corinthians 3:19-20 For the wisdom of **this** world is foolishness before God. For it is written, "*He is* the one who catches the wise in their craftiness"; [20] and again, "The Lord knows the reasonings of the wise, that they are useless."

ᖇᨓ

This world would have us believe that it is wise beyond all else out there. Now that is REAL FOOLISHNESS! When we take into account what is going on and what drives everything that goes on around the world, it doesn't take a very astute person to come to the conclusion that this world is short on wisdom and very long on foolishness. When idols, such as famous people, different animals, as well as money, power, fame, tarot cards, and horoscopes etc. have such prolific and rapt attention by all of us, we have to admit we are on a truly meaningless and worthless path. We want so badly to have meaning, but the meaning we want is for ourselves to be God and we're "hacked" that this is not the case!

How many friends or acquaintances have you watched throw their families, professions, even themselves under the bus for the simple reason of getting some notoriety or insidious desire met that is fleeting, short term, and worthless in the grand scheme of things? What are we doing watching these degrading and demeaning reality shows which have people reveling in the misfortunes of others so they can forget our own. What's with all the E.D. commercials, and who on earth cares how "has been" stars dance?

We strive after useless things while ignoring the most wise, most magnificent God Who created us. How can we escape this trap Satan puts before us day by day? The only possibility for us to do so is through Jesus Christ and increasing our fellowship with Him, as opposed to our fellowship with the world. If we are not establishing and growing in our relationship with Jesus, we have no hope of escaping the clutches of "this present darkness" spoken of in **Ephesians 6**.

Speaking of this phrase, Frank Peretti's classic – This Present Darkness – will give you insight into the spiritual warfare which is possibly and probably going on around each and every one of us 24 hours a day. It is a fictional book, but paints a very believable picture of what that warfare could look like. If you start it, it won't take you long to read it, I assure you.

> **1 Corinthians 2:6-8** Yet we do speak wisdom among those who are mature; a wisdom, however, not of **this** age, nor of the rulers of **this** age, who are passing away; [7] but we speak God's wisdom in a mystery, the hidden *wisdom*, which God predestined before the ages to our glory; [8] *the wisdom* which none of the rulers of **this** age has understood; for if

they had understood it, they would not
have crucified the Lord of glory;
∽⋆∽

The rulers of this age are the ones who are perishing and
passing away, like Satan. God alone has true wisdom which
will be there for the ages, eternity in fact. Yet we like to
think we have our act together and "know the program" as
another of my mentors liked to say. Do we really know what
"knowing the program" is? I would have to say that it is
realizing that God is God and we are not. It would be the
mature and reverent thing to do, to love Him, seek Him, and
worship Him in a manner that showed our awe and respectful
appreciation of the one true God of the universe. How much
we would benefit ourselves if we could but set our own
selfish desires to the side and delve into His Word and make
the time to spend with Him in prayer – real, sincere prayer.
Our lives would take on so much more meaning and truly
impact so many more of those we come into contact with.
But we can't seem to do this very well in our busy lives. It
takes a discipline which many of us don't have, because we
are on fast-forward mode, and just trying to "stay with the
pack" of those around us.

Satan, the ruler of this world and this age would have
us focused on wrongful priorities and motives. I have been
blessed since I was a teenager to ask for advice from those
who were older and wiser than I certainly knew I was. One of
the questions I have asked repeatedly of men with integrity
who were older than me, say in their sixties or seventies,
was this: "If you had it all to do over again, what would you

do differently, looking back on your life?" Almost without exception the answer is virtually the same from each one I've asked: "Mark, if I had it to do over again, I would have spent less time trying to build my business and make money, and more time with my wife and kids while the kids were home. Now, I have all the money I need, but the kids don't come around so much anymore and I regret the fact that I missed out on so much of their lives while they were growing up."

What a sad realization to have when all is said and done – that those things we thought were so very important at the time, turned out to be not as crucial as we had thought. In the end, we come to the conclusion that we've made decisions that have wasted valuable time and taken us from the truly meaningful things that were right under our noses. My son Joseph, who was eleven at the time, came in the bathroom last summer while I was shaving and asked me – "Dad, if you had it to do over again, would you choose to be a dentist?" The apple doesn't fall too far from the tree does it? That'll be good for him in some respects – bad in others I suppose. By the way, I'm trying to spend as much time as I can with my kids – while they're home.

This world lies to us so much, so often, and so forcefully that we succumb to its lies; and start believing them to be true. That's why we have to cling to His Word and spend time in it on a daily basis or we have no chance, NO CHANCE to be able to withstand the world's onslaught of our minds. If we can be obedient and have the discipline to stay the course in His Word, then and only then will our minds begin to receive the truth in a manner which will bring change; which brings us to our next verse:

> **Romans 12:1-2** I urge you therefore, brethren, by the mercies of God, to present your bodies a living and holy sacrifice, acceptable to God, *which is* your spiritual service of worship. ² And do not be conformed to **this** world, but be transformed by the renewing of your mind, that you may prove what the will of God is, that which is good and acceptable and perfect.
>
> ☜☞

This sacrifice of time in the Bible will bless us so very much, yet we don't see the blessings because we don't ever make the sacrifice. We are too busy! Too tired! Have too much other "stuff" to do. We all have the same amount of time and each of us needs to make the effort to carve out time to spend with Him and guard it as though our lives depended on it. And guess what? THEY DO!

We will have little success if we just expect to take in a sermon a week and not search into the heart and soul of His Word. We cannot attain and have a renewing of our mind without exercising it regularly in what we want it trained up in. I can speak to this because I have lived it. I can't help but believe that if we Christians would commit to spending 30 minutes a day in prayer and Bible study, we would have such a transformation of our churches it would be unbelievable. Imagine how you would feel if you started out each and every morning and the first rattle out of bed, spending 15 minutes in prayer and another 15 minutes in His Word. We would each start our days with so much more focus on Him and His will and a lot less of our focus would be on ourselves and our many worries and problems.

First, we have to start with ourselves; then as we interact with others, they would see the difference, ask how they could experience it, and the ripples would grow and grow, transforming not only our minds, but the entire world as well.

"This" is our commandment!

> **Matthew 22:36-40** "Teacher, which is the great commandment in the Law?" [37] And He said to him, "You shall love the LORD your God with all your heart, and with all your soul, and with all your mind. [38] This is the great and foremost commandment. [39] The second is like it, You shall love your neighbor as yourself. [40] On these two commandments depend the whole Law and the Prophets."

If we will first have the love of Christ in our hearts – then it can't help but be expressed and shown to those around us. The sooner we latch on to these two laws, the sooner we, through the power of the Holy Spirit, will have transformed and renewed minds and be able to impact those around us for Christ.

I have a patient who wore a lapel button into the office one day. I'm not sure if she wore it for everyone's benefit or especially for me, but the button said, Accept Your Greatness! She is an extremely nice and outgoing person and obviously knows I am a Christian by just walking into the office. I had asked her if she and her husband attended church anywhere and her response made it clear to me that they were not people of faith – at least faith in Jesus Christ. I believe the term "New Age" might be appropriate in this case, judging from the direction our conversations always took. Remember, I am not going to hammer her about her faith or lack of it. I do want to be a stepping stone and not a stumbling block for her. If I come on too strong and turn her off in her assessment of Christians, what good have I done for the Kingdom? I choose to show her the love of Christ in an unfailing manner, bend over backwards to serve her, and be accessible to her if and when she ever asks me anything regarding my faith. She may never ask me about my faith at all, and that is certainly fine as well.

One thing I am confident of is she has faith in something. We all do. Whether it is money, family, government, alcohol, New Age, mood rings, pet rocks, or lapel buttons, we all have faith in something or someone. The trouble is that most people's faith is misdirected due to the world's influence on them. You might be saying to yourself, "Man this guy is arrogant!" No, I'm not arrogant, I am a believer. I am a real life believer in the love of Christ, and I believe what He is saying in these verses.

Our love of God must take precedence in all our heart, soul, and mind, which is our command from Jesus Christ Himself. If we believe in ANYTHING else, we are the ones who are arrogant – arrogant for taking allegiance that rightfully and truly belongs only to the one true God, and distributing it to anything but Him.

So, back to my patient, I see my task as getting to know her better. I will have other opportunities to spend time with her, getting glimpses of where she is truly coming from and what she truly believes in, unless she decides to go to another dentist. If I come on too strong, I could drive her out of my practice and then she might not have another dentist who is a believer. She might end up dying worshiping that lapel button. It took me 28 years to finally acknowledge Jesus as my Lord who knows when and if anyone will come to Him – it may be on their very deathbed at the age of 101.

> **Romans 13:11** And **this** *do*, knowing the time, that it is already the hour for you to awaken from sleep; for now salvation is nearer to us than when we believed.
>
>

One thing is certain, each day that passes is one day less that we have to help those around us and be an influence on them for Christ. This verse in **Romans** comes right after Paul has reiterated in verse 9, "You shall love your neighbor as yourself."

William MacDonald, in his commentary, states about verse 11, "The time is short. The Dispensation of Grace is drawing to a close. The lateness of the hour demands that all lethargy and inactivity be put away."

There is a sense of urgency here. I sense it, do you? I think a lot of people do, they just don't know how to put their finger on it to recognize it for what it is. The uneasiness and angst going on around us is increasing daily. Which means the opportunities for us to minister to those around us is increasing as well, if we will but seize those opportunities. What if, when we go to heaven and are able to look back, we see the times that words were not spoken but should have been, the opportunities lost where we should have taken the time to speak to a loved one for Christ and didn't. I don't know that we will be able to do this, but what if? What if we look back and see a GRAND PUZZLE into which all these intricate pieces fit – a word here, a gesture there, a time of shared prayer over there – all these pieces fitting together in a great and wondrous kaleidoscope of minute, yet profoundly important events, making the puzzle complete.

However, a couple of the pieces are missing – and they were our pieces which we were to have contributed. Oh, in God's perfect plan, we all know that those pieces will not be left out – because His plan is perfect. What we may encounter though, is that we have lost out on many blessings we could have if we had only had our priorities in the right place. What if this book if it ever made it to print, impacted one and only one individual and helped that person to reach out to Christ. Would it have been worth the hours of effort, YOU BETCHA, YOU BETCHA, YOU BETCHA!

1 Corinthians 4:1 Let a man regard us in **this** manner, as servants of Christ, and stewards of the mysteries of God.

Understand, dear Reader, as Christians, we are servants and we are stewards – or we are not. We have a say in the matter. We can choose to be servants of those around us or we can say, "Hey, that's not MY problem, don't get me involved." We can choose to be stewards of our faith in Christ or we can push that faith aside, at any time, I might add.

What are we doing in regard to these two areas of our lives? What kind of servants are we to those in need, family, friends, acquaintances, coworkers, absolute strangers? We need to wake up. If we are not seeing needy people out there, we are not looking and are so absorbed in ourselves, we are blind to a dying and suffering world all around us. What kind of stewards are we being of our faith in Christ? Are we actively spending time with Him, seeking ways to serve His needs through our lives or have we put our faith up on a shelf to "maybe" take out and use at a later date.

Just a couple of weeks ago, I received an email from a very good friend I had contacted about the coming out of this book. I sent her the Introduction to read and her response was very enthusiastic. Keyea and I had not spoken to her in a while, so I thought maybe I should give Alice a call to see how she was doing.

You know how it is, "Should I bother her? Is it the right time to call? Maybe she's too busy to talk." We all come up with various and sundry excuses whether to bug someone or not. I elected to make the call, and am I glad I did.

When Alice picked up the phone and answered I told her I was grateful for her enthusiasm about the Introduction and thankful she would take the time to read it. She responded,

"Mark, I'm so glad you called! I really did enjoy what you wrote and I can't wait to read the rest of the book when it comes out!"

I asked her how she was doing, paused for her to answer, and that was all it took for the conversation to take on a very different tone than the enthusiasm expressed just moments earlier. "Mark, I'm really struggling with what all is going on in my life and the decisions I am being confronted with right now. I've taken a new job with more responsibility and have had to move in order to take the position." She hesitated and stammered a little, then said, " Mark, I really feel like my life has been a total failure. It really feels like I am in the "pits" and I don't know how to get out of them!"

I asked her how she had come to that conclusion and she just said she was feeling like her life was totally inadequate and had no real meaningful purpose to it. From there, I asked her if she would want to come down and spend a weekend with Keyea and me and visit about it. I spoke with Keyea and it turned out the very next weekend was about the only time we would have available for the next month or so.

Alice came down Saturday morning and spent that day and night visiting with Keyea and me, and went to church with us the next morning. Tears were shed, feelings were shared, and inadequacies reassessed in the context of what the Bible says. There was a good bit of laughter about old times as well. The next morning at church the message was about "Fear" and how debilitating it could be in our lives. It was the perfect message for the perfect recipient.

We went home to have lunch and visit before Alice was

going to have to head back to her home in East Texas. She told us she wanted the three of us to sit down and visit before she left, so we sat in the den and she shared something about the phone call last weekend and her visit to our home and church this weekend. Alice said she was so thankful for my call the previous Sunday because had I not made that call, she was contemplating taking her life that very afternoon. Through streams of tears, she stated that her evaluation of her life and its worth was at an all time low, and had I not made the phone call, she could well have made a very big mistake.

Keyea and I have both been praying for her and have asked her to seek further counseling in order to address the depression she is obviously in. We have both called her a couple of times this last week and she is at a better place than she was, but still recognizes she needs the help of a professional. I can only imagine what might have happened if that phone call had not been made. In retrospect, I don't think it was my idea to call at all – I think it was Him directing me to make that call to Alice.

"This" is what we want to avoid!

> **1 Peter 2:4-8**   [4] And coming to Him as to a living stone, rejected by men, but choice and precious in the sight of God,   [5] you also, as living stones, are being built up as a spiritual house for a holy priesthood, to offer up spiritual sacrifices acceptable to God through Jesus Christ.   [6] For *this* is contained in Scripture: "Behold I lay in Zion a choice

stone, a precious corner *stone*, And
he who believes in Him shall not be
disappointed." ⁷ This precious value,
then, is for you who believe. But for
those who disbelieve, "The stone which
the builders rejected, This became the
very corner *stone*," ⁸ and, "A stone
of stumbling and a rock of offense";
for they stumble because they are
disobedient to the word, and to **this**
doom they were also appointed.
∽

In these verses Peter is quoting **Isaiah 8:14** and they point
to Jesus Christ being a stumbling block for those who don't
believe in Him. I don't know how you feel about the last
part of this segment of Scripture, but it does seem that there
are some who are destined or appointed for destruction. This
is not something we, as loving and caring people, want to
acknowledge or give credence. But look closely and notice
why they are doomed. They are disobedient to His Word
and, as a result, disobedient to Him. We need to understand
that Jesus is our only hope and that He and He alone, is the
way of salvation for our lost souls.

I like what John MacArthur says in his commentary on
these verses: "To every human being, Christ is either the
means of salvation if they believe, or the means of judgment
if they reject the gospel. He is like a stone in the road that
causes a traveler to fall. Unbelief is their disobedience, since
the call of the gospel to repent and believe is a command
from God." Dr. MacArthur goes on to say: "These were not
appointed by God to disobedience and unbelief. Rather, these

were appointed to doom BECAUSE of their disobedience and unbelief." Lastly, he states: "Judgment on unbelief is as divinely appointed as salvation by faith."

You and I can avoid the "doom" scenario. How? We must repent of our sins, we must throw ourselves at the foot of His cross and ask for forgiveness, and we must look to Jesus as our only Savior and hope. Once we have placed our hope and faith in Him, then and only then does Jesus cease being a stumbling block for us – He then becomes the precious cornerstone in which we shall not be disappointed!

"This" is what our struggle is against!

> **Ephesians 6:12** For our struggle is not against flesh and blood, but against the rulers, against the powers, against the world forces of **this** darkness, against the spiritual *forces* of wickedness in the heavenly *places.*

If we don't find ourselves in a struggle with Satan, we can pretty well be assured we are probably in his clutches and don't even know it. The battle lines are drawn – they will not be taken away this side of heaven. Satan wants to own us. He wants us so bad, he can taste it. In the Scriptures, he is portrayed as a lion - **1 Peter 5:8 [8] Be of sober *spirit*, be on the alert. Your adversary, the devil, prowls about like a roaring lion, seeking someone to devour.** He longs for us to throw in the towel and succumb to his minions.

Once we are there and he has us in his grasp, he's off

to gather in another... and another... and another. Satan and his demons are myriad, as well as powerful. We do not want to underestimate their ability to ensnare us and wrap us up in their web of deceit which is so very tight, it is near impossible – dare I say, it is impossible – to escape save for the shed blood of Jesus Christ.

Paul gives us advice on what armor to put on in order to fight against these perpetrators of evil in **Ephesians 6:13-18**. The armor goes from the helmet of salvation to having our feet girded with the gospel of peace. Oh, and by the way, the weapon of offense in the battle is the sword of the Spirit, which is the Word of God. We can't wield the predominant weapon to be used against Satan if we never pick it up to read and study it.

This struggle of spiritual warfare is in us and around us whether we want to acknowledge it or not – it does not go away just because we say we don't believe in it. Don't think that reality is only what you can see, think, and feel. We are limited as to what we can comprehend about the spiritual world right now, but one day the veil will be pulled back to reveal a reality we only have fleeting evidences of in this life.

An example of this is when Elisha and his servant were getting ready for battle

> **2 Kings 6:15-17**   [15] Now when the attendant of the man of God had risen early and gone out, behold, an army with horses and chariots was circling the city. And his servant said to him, "Alas, my master! What shall we do?"   [16] So he answered, "Do not fear, for those who

are with us are more than those who are with them." [17] Then Elisha prayed and said, "O LORD, I pray, open his eyes that he may see." And the LORD opened the servant's eyes, and he saw; and behold, the mountain was full of horses and chariots of fire all around Elisha.

Yes, my friend, the battle lines are definitely drawn in this world. Which cause are you going to serve and what are you going to do in regard to that service? This is the question to which all of us will have to give an account one day. Just remember, time is short and getting shorter each day. And by the way, as Ron Presswood would say: "This Ain't No Dress Rehearsal Baby!"

CHAPTER 10 - CHAOS

Keyea asked me what chapter I was writing on in the book this morning and I told her I was starting the Chaos chapter. "Man, you could write a whole book on that one topic alone!" she said. The truth is, one could! We have a lot of chaos going on in and around our world today and it's actually been going on for quite a while.

When I mention the book to friends, they always ask what the title is. When I tell them, they say, "Well that is sure an appropriate title for these times." The real truth is that this title has been appropriate for all times, just to slightly different degrees. You see, this fallen world has been on a collision course with the wrath of God since the great fall in the Garden of Eden. These times that we live in seem much more chaotic to us because we are right in the middle of them, living out our lives and thinking the world is going to hell in a hand-basket. It is and it has been all along.

I'm sorry to have to ask you to read this, but then again, I'm not. This troubling, but true, text out of Isaiah should chill us to our very core as it points to the ultimate end of our world as we know it. If this doesn't bring you to your knees in repentance, I don't know what will, this side of heaven.

Chaos is the word and annihilation is the end for those who don't repent and seek His forgiveness and grace. Oh, and that is not annihilation to hell to party with the other partying sinners. Oh contraire!

"Chaos" is and has been the course of our world!

Isaiah 24:1–23 Behold, the LORD lays the earth waste, devastates it, distorts its surface, and scatters its inhabitants. ² And the people will be like the priest, the servant like his master, the maid like her mistress, the buyer like the seller, the lender like the borrower, the creditor like the debtor. ³ The earth will be completely laid waste and completely despoiled, for the LORD has spoken this word. ⁴ The earth mourns *and* withers, the world fades *and* withers, the exalted of the people of the earth fade away. ⁵ The earth is also polluted by its inhabitants, for they transgressed laws, violated statutes, broke the everlasting covenant. ⁶ Therefore, a curse devours the earth, and those who live in it are held guilty. Therefore, the inhabitants of the earth are burned, and few men are left. ⁷ The new wine mourns, The vine decays, All the merry-hearted sigh. ⁸ The gaiety of tambourines ceases, The noise of revelers stops, The gaiety of the harp ceases. ⁹ They do not drink wine with song; Strong drink is bitter to those who drink it. ¹⁰ The city of **chaos** is broken down; Every house is shut up so that none may enter. ¹¹ There is an outcry in the streets concerning the wine; All joy turns to gloom. The gaiety of the earth is banished. ¹² Desolation is left in the city, And the gate is battered to ruins. ¹³ For thus it will be in the midst of the earth among the peoples, As the shaking of an olive tree, As the gleanings when the grape harvest is over. ¹⁴ They raise their voices, they shout for joy. They cry out from the west concerning the majesty of the LORD. ¹⁵ Therefore glorify the LORD in the east, The name of the LORD, the God of Israel In the coastlands of the sea. ¹⁶ From the ends of the earth we hear songs, "Glory to the Righteous One," But I say, "Woe to me! Woe to me! Alas for me! The treacherous deal treacherously, And the treacherous deal very treacherously." ¹⁷ Terror and pit and snare Confront you, O inhabitant of the earth. ¹⁸ Then it will be that he who flees the report of disaster will fall into the pit, And he who climbs out of the pit will be caught in the snare; For the windows above are opened, and the foundations of the earth shake. ¹⁹ The earth is broken asunder, The earth is split through, The earth is shaken violently. ²⁰ The earth reels to and fro like a drunkard, And it totters like a shack, For its transgression is heavy upon it, And it will fall, never to rise again. ²¹ So it will happen in that day, That the LORD will punish the host of heaven, on high, And the kings of the earth, on earth. ²² And they will be gathered together *Like* prisoners in the dungeon, And will be confined in prison; And after many days they will be punished. ²³ Then the moon will be abashed and the sun ashamed, For the LORD of hosts will reign on Mount Zion and in Jerusalem, And *His* glory will be before His elders.

∽ᴗ✧

Now THAT'S some CHAOS! Man I feel great! How about you? NOT!

Chapters 13-24 in **Isaiah** deal with God's judgment on a perverse and wicked world – our world. We are in the middle of what some feel and think are the end times for our civilization. You are right – people have been claiming this is the case since Jesus rose and went up into heaven on a cloud. The difference may be that 2000 years have transpired, a lot of prophesy in the Bible has come true, and some would say that all the required prophesy spoken of in the Scriptures has come to pass with nothing else needing to happen to usher in the second coming of Christ.

We mustn't get too wrapped up and focused on the time of Christ's return because no one, NO ONE, knows when that day will be. But it is not a question of "when" that a lot of people are concerned with. To a lot of folks the mistaken question they have is "if" it will happen. I can understand their doubts about all this prophecy muckety-muck because I used to be right there with them. I'm not in that camp now, however.

I don't think it is a question of "if," only of "when" Jesus Christ will come for His Second Coming. Those who have no faith don't want to acknowledge that it is even a possibility. They believe we all die and that's it for this life, there is nothing afterward. Remember me saying everybody has faith in "something?" We all do, whether it is faith in ourselves, money, a god, death, or whatever, we each have faith in something. Those who don't believe that the Bible is true just have their faith vested in some other "something."

There is a great deal of that in this world we inhabit, huh?

> ¹ Behold, the LORD lays the earth waste, devastates it, distorts its surface, and scatters its inhabitants.

Do you remember when the people of the world tried to build a tower to heaven, the tower of Babel? It is recorded in **Genesis** chapter 11. Anyway, the people decided to erect a tower so they could make a name for themselves and put themselves on par with God. We don't want to miss the fact that God didn't direct the people to do this, **they** decided to do it. In other words, they wanted to make themselves God.

Kind of sounds like the devil again, doesn't it? God didn't approve of this plan, so He confused their language and scattered them to the ends of the earth. Mankind has been rejecting God and His sovereignty since the bite into the forbidden fruit. It is at the core of our soul and we can't shake it, can't deny it, and cannot overcome it without Jesus Christ as our Savior to free us from it.

Once language barriers were in the picture and peoples were scattered, men and women in different pockets of the world began coming up with, dreaming up, and scheming up their own ideas of religion and what to worship. They couldn't just trust in His plan, so with their own plan, they set out misleading their people down wrong paths which led to nowhere but power, greed, and chaos.

This chaos further leads us to verse 2.

> ² And the people will be like the priest, the servant like his master, the maid like her mistress, the buyer like the seller, the lender like the borrower, the creditor like the debtor.
> ⁕

It is like Lee Iacocca speaks of in his book – <u>Where Have All the Leaders Gone?</u> It seems the true men of integrity have "left the building" as far as our nation is concerned. With so few leaders and all the chaos, the field is going to be "white for the harvest" as Jesus stated in **John 4:35**.

A lot of people in the Church – devout people who study the Word of God and have a fervent prayer life – say that we, as a nation, are reaping what we've sown in our rejection of prayer from our schools, separation of church and state, as well as succumbing to those who would have us take all reference to God out of every part of our nation's heritage and history. This movement seems to have its most prevalent roots in the 60s. That's when prayer was taken out of schools, "love ins" were in vogue, women's lib got its start, Vietnam war protests raged, drug use became the norm, and progressive thinking was the new thing.

> ³ The earth will be completely laid waste and completely despoiled, for the LORD has spoken this word. ⁴ The earth mourns *and* withers, the world fades *and* withers, the exalted of the people of the earth fade away.
> ⁕

Yes "the exalted of the people of the earth fade away" – our nation was once the most faithful Christian nation on earth – with that faith was a power to help rid the landscape of some of the most despicable inhumane tyrants in the history of the world. We are on our way to becoming a "shell" of the nation we once were and I'm convinced a lot of it comes from our rejection of our Lord and not having a strong faith in Him. Who knows where we will eventually end up – only God knows, but it's not looking pretty right now.

> **5 The earth is also polluted by its inhabitants, for they transgressed laws, violated statutes, broke the everlasting covenant.**

We have certainly done a great job of this – in fact we have excelled at it. Not only were we rejecting God more in the 60s, we were flat out rebelling against anything we could get our hands on. If it stood for good morals and had a conservative bent to it, it wasn't only rejected and trashed, it was demonized as old-fashioned, irrelevant, and downright anti-modern. "DOWN WITH THE ESTABLISHMENT!" was the mantra of that period and by-golly, not only the establishment suffered, the entire culture of conservative Christian morals and values started being chipped away – and in huge chunks, I might add. "Flower power" and "free love" replaced God and Country.

> **6 Therefore, a curse devours the earth, and those who live in it are held guilty. Therefore, the inhabitants of the earth**

are burned, and few men are left.

That's right – the curse is devouring the earth we live in and we stand guilty. We are guilty of so much, it defies anyone to try to start naming off all the ways. I'll just mention a few:

- How are our families holding up through all this?
- How many blended families from so many divorces?
- How many abortions?
- How many births out of wedlock?
- How many fatherless children?
- Is marriage only between a man and a woman?
- Should we legalize marijuana?
- How's that porn industry goin' for ya?
- Did we have this many pedophiles before the advent of the internet?
- You better get those Ten Commandments out of that public building!
- Don't spank that kid of yours, it is child abuse!

We are cursed with so many curses, we can't even identify them all. Yes, Satan's myriad of demons are having a field day, and our country is right in the middle of it.

> **⁷ The new wine mourns, The vine decays, All the merry-hearted sigh. ⁸ The gaiety of tambourines ceases, The noise of revelers stops, The gaiety of the harp ceases. ⁹ They do not drink wine with song; Strong drink is bitter**

to those who drink it. ¹⁰ The city of chaos is broken down; Every house is shut up so that none may enter.

⮑⥀

Our country is "the city of chaos." You can feel the angst and trepidation out there every day. It is as though we are going through the motions, all the while knowing that something very catastrophic is about to happen. People are buying guns, extra food, generators, gold bullion, hording cash, building gates to guard their driveways. People are hunkering down and holing-up.

We don't know our neighbors like we used to. Technology has hampered our relationships and made them less deep and meaningful. Rather than speak with someone on the phone or in person, we text them and don't even have to respond to them if we don't want to. Caller ID allows us to "turn-off" those we want to be rid of anytime we want to. When we do talk, we speak in whispers as we are, for the first time in my life that I can remember, fearful that someone might be listening in on our conversations.

Yes, the "vine decays" and the "gaiety...ceases" as everyone is seeing our country being ripped up, shattered with debt, and class warfare propagated. Don't think the race card isn't being played either, it definitely is! We seem to be swiftly approaching critical mass in many ways and on many fronts.

¹¹ There is an outcry in the streets concerning the wine; All joy turns to gloom. The gaiety of the earth is

banished. [12] Desolation is left in the city, And the gate is battered to ruins. [13] For thus it will be in the midst of the earth among the peoples, As the shaking of an olive tree, As the gleanings when the grape harvest is over.

ᜢ᜶ᜢ

How's that infrastructure working for ya? Our country is awash in infrastructure breaking down and decaying, dilapidated bridges, broken down roads, no new power plants or refineries built in years. We have antiquated FAA equipment using tubes instead of the latest computer circuitry for goodness sakes! Everything those in control get their hands on and have control of is broken down, inefficient, and run by inept people with little concern for a balanced budget.

The imposed bureaucratic red tape and regulations stifle our ability to get things even done, much less get them done right! The environmentalist wackos want to fly in their private jets, but don't want to allow the common folk to drive a pickup truck. They hold our country hostage with so-called "global warming", which is refuted by just as many, if not more, scientists than those that buy into the concept. For cryin' out loud, the bread basket in California, where much of our produce comes from, has been sitting idle for two years because of an endangered 2-inch minnow. It is now a dustbowl. But I guess the minnows are doing okay.

Alas, I do fear that our "harvest is over." It sure does seem that our nation has turned a corner and the new direction doesn't look like it is going to be a joyful path.

> ¹⁴ They raise their voices, they shout for joy. They cry out from the west concerning the majesty of the LORD.
> ¹⁵ Therefore glorify the LORD in the east, The name of the LORD, the God of Israel In the coastlands of the sea.
> ¹⁶ From the ends of the earth we hear songs, "Glory to the Righteous One," But I say, "Woe to me! Woe to me! Alas for me! The treacherous deal treacherously, And the treacherous deal very treacherously." ¹⁷ Terror and pit and snare Confront you, O inhabitant of the earth.

The treacherous do deal treacherously with those they claim to serve. Our country's leaders claim to serve the down and out and the poor. The taxes they are proposing and passing through the legislature are going to put so much of a higher tax burden on the lower income segment of America, it is amazing!

As much as I may disagree with our leaders, they are in office, so I am praying for them. Do you know what I am praying for? I'm praying that the Holy Spirit would convict them and draw them to a saving faith in Jesus Christ. It seems that may be the only way to get them off of their greedy, self-serving, and treacherous agenda, and back to what we elect them to do – serve with the least amount of government possible.

[18] Then it will be that he who flees the report of disaster will fall into the pit, And he who climbs out of the pit will be caught in the snare; For the windows above are opened, and the foundations of the earth shake. [19] The earth is broken asunder, The earth is split through, The earth is shaken violently. [20] The earth reels to and fro like a drunkard, And it totters like a shack, For its transgression is heavy upon it, And it will fall, never to rise again.

~⌀~

Our transgressions are heavy upon us; wouldn't you agree? Listen dear reader, I am not some wacko-zealot revolutionist, but some are saying it is possible we could be headed for unprecedented civil unrest. I hear many people who say they feel our country could go into a downward spiral from this point as well. A patient told me today that he felt as if our country was on a roller-coaster and you can hear the clinking on the track, implying the coaster is moving up the great mountain of a track and getting ready to cascade in a free-for-all of confusion and destruction.

Now hear me out on this, I don't remember any of us talking this way just 1-2 years ago; but then I started to hear rumblings of it, and now it feels as if the rumblings are getting louder and louder and that the crisis could possibly come about. I pray it doesn't, but it truly does feel as if we are living in uncharted territory in the country we feel blessed to be a part of. Others would say we are getting what we deserve as a nation.

> ²¹ **So it will happen in that day, That the LORD will punish the host of heaven, on high, And the kings of the earth, on earth.** ²² **And they will be gathered together *Like* prisoners in the dungeon, And will be confined in prison; And after many days they will be punished.** ²³ **Then the moon will be abashed and the sun ashamed, For the LORD of hosts will reign on Mount Zion and in Jerusalem, And *His* glory will be before His elders.**
>
> ∽

"That day" is very interesting to Christians, as it should be to unbelievers as well. This day sounds like a day of judgment for all, both for those of the spiritual world and those of this world. The question for all of us is, "What if these events going on in our world at this time are pointing to that day coming sooner than later?" Again, none of us truly know, but I felt compelled to write this book as a wake-up call to try to help people think about what their true purpose is; as well as to help them be exposed to the trueness of their faith in Christ.

In those last days, it is apparent and emphasized that Christ's second coming is unexpected and swift – that it catches people off-guard and unaware. In fact, it is evident that everyone is carrying on as usual in their daily life just as **Matthew 24** and **Luke 17** predict.

The fewer of us who are deceived, the better, in my mind, wouldn't you agree? I have been exposed through my dental practice, my teaching, and my observations in daily life to the overwhelming conclusion that there are many misguided and confused people out there looking for something to fill the void they can't identify in their lives. That void can only be filled with one thing that is going to satisfy its insatiable cravings, the love of Jesus Christ. Without this love of, submission to, and faith in the One True Savior, there is no possible way to satisfy and fill the void.

If I asked you if you saw people out there searching for meaning and making poor decisions in their quest of it, I think most of you would agree that this is the case – in spades! Part of my job description, as I see it, is that if these writings can help answer questions for some out there searching, by helping them to come to Christ and scrutinize their real faith or lack of it, that is a good thing.

There is an escape from the chaos and you and I can have that escape now and forever if we will just submit to Him, pick up our cross daily, and follow Christ. We must follow Jesus – the "chaos breaker."

CHAPTER 11 - !

Finally, we are at the feel-good part of the book. Sorry it took so long. If we all would care to admit it, we love to rejoice. It makes us feel good all the way down to the tips of our fingers and even to our toes. When was the last time you and I really rejoiced over anything? Probably it was too long a time ago.

What does your soul rejoice in? Do we rejoice in anything at all? These are good questions which need serious thought and reflection, and we need to make the time to do so. Have you noticed a common theme and thread throughout this book? Intertwined throughout it is the issue of TIME!

Recently, while I was teaching, I had lunch with three dentists. We had a discussion about their practices and what they wanted to try to address to help them be more effective in their communication with their patients. On our walk back from lunch we were discussing this book and where I was in the process of getting it published. Steve asked me a question I have been asked a lot while I've been writing this book. He said, "Mark, where do you get the time to write a book – I know you're as busy with your family and practice and all that goes with it as I am?"

I explained, "You know it is a funny thing about time and when you are using it to serve your Lord and Savior. That thing is – I feel like He multiplies it for me – enabling me to spend time on what is truly meaningful as it comes across my path." How about you? Do you have a lot of extra time to do what you know is truly meaningful for His Kingdom? Or do you, like I still do at times, waste precious time doing meaningless stuff – for whatever reason?

Besides our health, time is one of the most precious commodities we have. There's another funny thing about time – we don't know how much of it we have on this earth, but we all have the same amount of it each and every day. All you and I get is 24 hours and that's it. How would you feel if I told you that you can have more joy in your 24 hours tomorrow than you did today? Would you want that joy?

The truth is, there are some people whose only happiness each day comes from being miserable. What a sad life to struggle through! Not only are they miserable – they get to share that misery with all those they come in contact with throughout their 24 hours.

What does your life exclaim to those around you each day? This is an honest and very important question we all should think about. How we answer it portrays our outlook on our lives, and gives indication of the truth we can come to grips with about ourselves.

At the post-graduate dental institute I've attended and taught at over the last 30 years, there is a Cross of Dentistry which is espoused and shared. The four tips of the cross are described as:

Know Yourself
Know the Patient
Know Your Work
Apply Your Knowledge

Which of these four do you think is the toughest one to work through for most people? Good guess, the Know Yourself part. Do you remember when I spoke earlier of people who I said are "living the lie?" A lot of that is because they have not spent much time, if any, reflecting and figuring out who they really are at their core. Let me illustrate with a diagram. By the way, this is courtesy of Dr. Presswood again.

When we see ourselves as being one way and others see us differently from what we think we are, there is disparity and more potential for discord. An example would be a person who says to himself, "You know, I am really a generous and giving person, and I exude good feelings and warmth to all those I come in contact with."

The first thing about this statement is that it may be true about you, but it is definitely not true about me! So, say this person really feels this way about themselves. BUT, say that those they associate with each day are saying, "Man, that so and so is so tight with a penny, he squeezes the copper out of it! Not only that, he's so crass and cold, I can hardly bear being around him!"

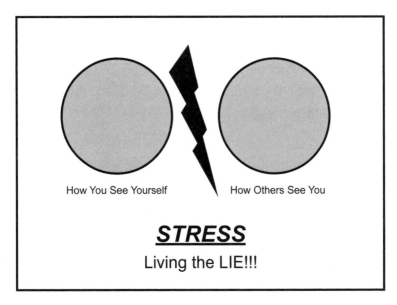

How You See Yourself   How Others See You

STRESS
Living the LIE!!!

Now if the observer is correct in his assessment of this individual, then this individual is truly "living the lie." What he thinks about himself is not reality – not even close to it! He rationalizes and morphs his thoughts about himself and sees himself in a wrong context.

This disparity between what this person believes about himself and what others truly think about him can and usually does create stress in this person's life in proportion to the amount of the discrepancy.

It fits right in with these verses - **2 Thessalonians 2:9-12 The coming of the lawless one will be in accordance with the work of Satan displayed in all kinds of counterfeit miracles, signs and wonders, [10] and in every sort of evil that deceives those who are perishing. They perish because they refused to love the truth and so be saved. [11] For this reason God sends them a powerful delusion so that they will believe the lie [12] and so that all will be**

condemned who have not believed the truth but have delighted in wickedness.

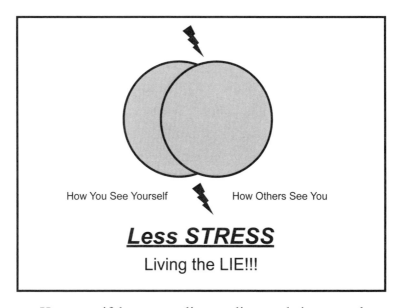

How You See Yourself   How Others See You

<u>Less STRESS</u>
Living the LIE!!!

However, if the way we live our lives and view ourselves is overlapped by the way others see us, then the amount of overlap of these two circles can give us an idea as to how much we are lying or being truthful to ourselves. The more they overlap, the more congruent are our lives and the less stress we will probably have because there is more consistency of our actions with who we truly are. Plus, we don't have to worry about exaggerating or lying, because we are being truthful with others and with ourselves. The truly hard part in all of this is "the getting to know ourselves part."

Are you confused yet? Don't be. There is a way to get in touch with who we are and it doesn't require horoscopes, séances, or the ever popular self-help books. It requires

TIME and His Book, the Bible. Of all the things I have done and tried over these last 29 years of my life, nothing has had more of an impact on how well I have gotten to know myself than spending time in His Word and time with Him in prayer.

When we expose ourselves to His Word on a daily basis, it cannot help but impact us and help us to know who we truly are. Studying the Bible has helped me to look at my life in what I feel is the proper context – according to my God's account of it. Yes, the Bible not only reveals my depraved, sinful state, it also radiates my glorious spiritual state and position of being a fellow heir of Jesus Christ, for eternity – no matter what.

Now what could be better news than that? NOTHING! No matter what goes on in this world and in this life (which is but a "breath" in the scope of eternity), I and my family will spend eternity with our Lord God and His Saints. There is no more joyful place to be assured of and to be certain of! NONE!

The more our lives resemble the next diagram, the more congruent we are with Jesus' will as well as having our minds transformed into having His outlook and servant attitude toward others. No, we will never be perfect this side of heaven; but if we don't lie to ourselves, we can start on the sanctification process and allow Christ to change us more and more into His image.

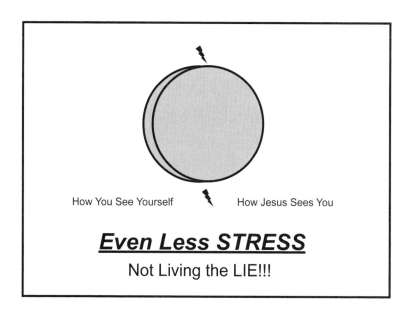

How You See Yourself   How Jesus Sees You

Even Less STRESS
Not Living the LIE!!!

I know, I know, some would say that there are different viewpoints and yes, there are.

M. Scott Peck in his book <u>The Road Less Traveled</u> summed the whole book up in the first sentence and it was only three words long – "Life is difficult!" He states that once you can accept that premise, you can move on to struggle your way through life and He is right, you CAN go through life that way, which a lot of people do.

But there is a better way, the best way, the Way of Jesus Christ. As I stated before, it is the Only True Way to eternity in heaven. This is the premise we should live our lives by. When we accept this premise, that we have our faith in Jesus Christ, then we will truly be able to get to know ourselves, get to know others, and help them to get to know Jesus as well. At long last when all is said and done, we will be able to praise Him and be with Him and the other saints forever.

Beyond the chaos and trials of this world we can rejoice in our God and Savior, for we know He is the ULTIMATE VICTOR!

In the next few pages I will give you more Scriptures than commentary and I do so for good reason. God's statements about joy and rejoicing are much, much more real and impactful than any commentary I might espouse. So sit back, take your time, real time – don't be rushed – and meditate on God's comments on rejoicing in Him.

Psalm 35:9-10 Then my soul will rejoice in the LORD and delight in his salvation. **¹⁰ My whole being will exclaim, "Who is like you, O LORD? You rescue the poor from those too strong for them, the poor and needy from those who rob them."**

We cannot help but feel better about ourselves and about those around us if we avail ourselves to having a true friendship and relationship with Christ. After all, even if this world beats us down, chews us up, and spits us out, we know the final outcome. Are you being taken advantage of, oppressed, and feeling there is no relief in sight? Come to Jesus, He alone can help you with your plight. Others may assist you and give you temporary respite, but only Jesus can give you respite forever, and He will do it – if you but ask.

Isaiah 61:10   I will rejoice greatly in

> the LORD, My soul will exult in my God; For He has clothed me with garments of salvation, He has wrapped me with a robe of righteousness, As a bridegroom decks himself with a garland, And as a bride adorns herself with her jewels.

Yes, through studying His Word we will see that all our efforts are as "filthy rags," but He clothes us in His righteousness, and turns those filthy rags into wonderful raiment to behold!

> **Deuteronomy 32:43** Rejoice, O nations, *with* His people; For He will avenge the blood of His servants, And will render vengeance on His adversaries, And will atone for His land *and* His people.

We don't have to get our revenge on those who wrong us – He will take care of that for us. He will help us to exercise patience and perseverance in the presence of trials and suffering.

> **Psalm 31:7-8** I will rejoice and be glad in Thy loving kindness, Because Thou hast seen my affliction; Thou hast known the troubles of my soul, ⁸ And Thou hast not given me over into the hand of the enemy; Thou hast set my feet in a large place.

The closer we are to Him, the more we will be able to feel His loving kindness and find rest in it. Though the trials we will have this side of heaven may seem to overwhelm us at times, Jesus will never give us more than we can bear (**1 Corinthians 10:13**).

Psalm 32:11 Be glad in the LORD and rejoice, you righteous ones, And shout for joy, all you who are upright in heart.

He will make us upright in heart if we will but spend time with Him in prayer and in His Word. If we have the discipline to do so, Jesus will give us joy unimaginable which will be evident to all those around us – for we can't help but share it.

Psalm 35:9 And my soul shall rejoice in the LORD; It shall exult in His salvation.

Psalm 35:27-28 Let them shout for joy and rejoice, who favor my vindication; And let them say continually, "The LORD be magnified, Who delights in the prosperity of His servant." [28] **And my tongue shall declare Thy righteousness And Thy praise all day long.**

**Psalm 70:4 Let all who seek Thee rejoice
and be glad in Thee; And let those who
love Thy salvation say continually, "Let
God be magnified."**

**Philippians 4:4 Rejoice in the Lord
always; again I will say, rejoice!**

With an upright heart, we shall not be able to help
ourselves from exalting Him and exclaiming Him to others.
We will have a passion to share His gospel with those we
come into contact with each and every day. We will be
compelled to look for opportunities to visit with a lost and
dying world of people around us.

**2 Corinthians 13:11 Finally, brethren,
rejoice, be made complete, be
comforted, be like-minded, live in
peace; and the God of love and peace
shall be with you.**

Jesus will help us to be transformed more and more
into His likeness; in fact, He will make us complete. That
completeness will become more and more evident as our
lives become more and more in tune with His will for us.

**1 Thessalonians 5:16-18 Rejoice
always; [17] pray without ceasing; [18]
in everything give thanks; for this is
God's will for you in Christ Jesus.**

If we will but put our trust in Him, He will give us the ability to be thankful and rejoice in Him and the blessings He bestows on us. Our prayer lives will expand to new levels and effectiveness we have never experienced before.

> **1 Peter 1:6-9 In this you greatly rejoice, even though now for a little while, if necessary, you have been distressed by various trials, ⁷ that the proof of your faith, *being* more precious than gold which is perishable, even though tested by fire, may be found to result in praise and glory and honor at the revelation of Jesus Christ; ⁸ and though you have not seen Him, you love Him, and though you do not see Him now, but believe in Him, you greatly rejoice with joy inexpressible and full of glory, ⁹ obtaining as the outcome of your faith the salvation of your souls.**

Receiving Jesus as our Lord does not mean we will not be distressed by trials. In reality we may have more difficult trials, but that is okay. No matter what we are confronted with on this earth, we know the "outcome of our faith" will be "the salvation of our soul."

> **1 Peter 4:12-14 Beloved, do not be surprised at the fiery ordeal among you, which comes upon you for your testing, as though some strange thing were happening to you; ¹³ but to the degree that you share the sufferings of**

> **Christ, keep on rejoicing; so that also at the revelation of His glory, you may rejoice with exultation. ¹⁴ If you are reviled for the name of Christ, you are blessed, because the Spirit of glory and of God rests upon you.**
>
> ∽⋌∾

As a matter of fact, our true faith in Christ will probably lead to our paying a price and even suffering with Him. The amazing thing is He gives us the ability to rejoice in that suffering.

We may at times feel that the trials we are confronted with on our walk of faith are insurmountable; but we can rest on the fact that Jesus draws us closer to Himself through those trials and that, with perseverance and faith in Him alone, we will be as He is – VICTORIOUS!

> **Revelation 19:6-7 And I heard, as it were, the voice of a great multitude and as the sound of many waters and as the sound of mighty peals of thunder, saying, "Hallelujah! For the Lord our God, the Almighty, reigns. ⁷ Let us rejoice and be glad and give the glory to Him, for the marriage of the Lamb has come and His bride has made herself ready."**
>
> ∽⋌∾

These are the voices we want to be a part of. It will be utterly amazing to be in heaven with God the Father, God the Son, and God the Holy Spirit, where all our questions will be answered and all our trials not even remembered, living in joy unparalleled by anything we have experienced here on this earth.

My prayer for you!

> **Colossians 1:9-14   For this reason also, since the day we heard *of it*, we have not ceased to pray for you and to ask that you may be filled with the knowledge of His will in all spiritual wisdom and understanding,   ¹⁰ so that you may walk in a manner worthy of the Lord, to please *Him* in all respects, bearing fruit in every good work and increasing in the knowledge of God;   ¹¹ strengthened with all power, according to His glorious might, for the attaining of all steadfastness and patience; joyously   ¹² giving thanks to the Father, who has qualified us to share in the inheritance of the saints in light.   ¹³ For He delivered us from the domain of darkness, and transferred us to the kingdom of His beloved Son,   ¹⁴ in whom we have redemption, the forgiveness of sins.**

Do you remember me remarking several times in this book what "my" question was? The question was and is, "Why are we here?" In 1990, some eight years after I had seriously started to spend time with my Lord in His Word, I received the answer to my question. I now KNOW – why I am here. Do you?

Here is why I am here: <u>I am here to serve the Lord Who sent me, to serve those He sends to me with reverence and humility, for His glory</u>! That my friend is why I am here. I want to ask you now – why are you here? It's a very good question – can you answer it?

Russ Massey shared something with us in BSF years ago which has stuck with me and ties right in with the answer to my "question." Russ said, "You know, when you get right down to it, here's what I think we are here to do….We are here on this earth and we are in enemy territory. While we are here, we have people who cross our paths and we are to get to know them. As we get to know them - who they are, where they come from, what they believe - we are then able to ascertain where they are on their walk of faith or lack of it. Now knowing them and where they are on their path, we can then plant seeds, ask questions, be there, and pray for them in order to help them to take either their first step of faith to Jesus Christ or their next step of faith in Jesus Christ. And then their next step, and then their next step….. All the while, during the process, guess what? They in different ways are helping US….to take OUR next step….on OUR road to sanctification."

I think Russ hit the nail on the head with this word picture. When we do GET RIGHT DOWN TO IT – we are here to be "stepping stones" and not "stumbling blocks" to those we come in contact with in this world. Let's be those "stepping stones" to all who cross our paths.

My "challenge" to you!

Have you taken your "first" step toward a saving faith in Jesus Christ as your Lord and Savior? After all, He is the only Way UP. If you have not taken that step, why not? Is your pride getting in the way? Don't let pride keep you from the one and only Way "UP." It will be for eternity.

If you have taken that first step, what is your next step on your walk of faith? Have you even thought about your next step? What is it that the Lord wants you to do to deepen your relationship with Him? It might be as simple as setting aside 5-10 minutes of quiet time with Him each morning. That 5-10 minutes can make a HUGE difference and have a GREAT impact on your entire life.

I want you to know that I had no idea I was going to be writing this book. Likewise I had no idea that you would be reading it. I am now at the end of something I feel was more thrust upon me than planned out. This being the case, I cannot imagine that God would have me write this without one person reading it – but then again, maybe He just wanted me to grow by "fleshing out" my thoughts on Him, who knows. But since it has been written and if anyone reads these pages, I want you to know that I am praying for you. And I want you to have joy, the only true joy that matters, the joy of knowing you are one with Jesus Christ and that that joy will be there forever and ever. Amen!

My friend, no matter who you are, no matter how much stuff or power you have, no matter how much you feel like you are in control of your own destiny, you have nothing that can compare with the joy of the day you realize you have truly "died and gone to heaven!" Or, on the other hand, absolutely nothing will be more excruciatingly painful, more hopeless, or more agonizing, than realizing you have rejected the One True Way of Jesus Christ when it was right there in front of you all your life. Yet here you are condemned, doomed, and with no possible hope of ever getting across the chasm, where you know Jesus and His saints are rejoicing, FOREVER. Which will it be? You are making a choice whether you want to admit it or not.

So, Which Way Is Up? From Amongst All This Chaos! Our time is shorter today than it was yesterday and the eternity we will spend is ever closer each day. Time is short, but eternity is forever. So in closing, I would like to leave you with three passages to consider:

> **Deuteronomy 30:19-20 I call heaven and earth to witness against you today, that I have set before you life and death, the blessing and the curse. So choose life in order that you may live, you and your descendants, 20 by loving the LORD your God, by obeying His voice, and by holding fast to Him; for this is your life and the length of your days, that you may live in the land which the LORD swore to your fathers, to Abraham, Isaac, and Jacob, to give them.**

And as Jesus Himself states:

Matthew 6:33 [33] **"But seek first His kingdom and His righteousness; and all these things shall be added to you."**

∽✕∾

John 16:33 [33] **"These things I have spoken to you, that in Me you may have peace. In the world you have tribulation, but take courage; I have overcome the world."**

∽✕∾

STUDY GUIDE

- **Chapter 1 – Which**

  1. Which "choices" have you been making that you feel you should change?

  2. How is the "busyness" in your life hampering your effectiveness in doing really meaningful tasks that impact yourself and others?

  3. Which foundation do you find yourself mainly building on – rock or sand?

  4. Which family members or friends do you know that you should start "planting seeds" with to help them take a step of faith?

  5. Which name do you feel is above all names?

- **Chapter 2 – Way**

  1. Do you feel there are many "ways" to heaven?

  2. How did the five attributes of hell impact you?

  3. Are you entering on the narrow gate (few) or are you on the wide and broad way that (many) are on?

  4. Do you have a real and meaningful relationship with Jesus – does He know you?

  5. Can we earn our way into heaven?

- **Chapter 3 – Is**

  1. How is "relativism, tolerance, and progressive thinking" impacting our society?
  2. Have you ever told God what He should do?
  3. Are you "abiding in Christ?"
  4. Are you attending church regularly?
  5. Can you explain to people why bad things can still happen even while God is in control?
  6. Are you ashamed of Jesus?
  7. Will God judge the sins of mankind?

- **Chapter 4 – Up**

  1. Do you believe Jesus was raised up and resurrected?
  2. Do you believe Jesus has all authority?
  3. Are you prepared to stand alone before God the Father?
  4. What are you doing to be "trained up?"
  5. Are you in the "PITS" or at the "PINNACLE?"
  6. Do you get a "FIT" award each day?

- **Chapter 5 - ?**

  1. Do you ask good questions? …such as????
  2. Have you ever asked anyone about their faith or where they go to church?
  3. Do you have Scriptures to share with others or tracts

to give them if the need arises?

4. Who do you say that Jesus is?

5. Are you ready to give this answer to God the Father?

- **Chapter 6 – From**

    1. Where are you "from?"

    2. Have you studied evolution or the origin of the Bible?

    3. Are we people as a whole – depraved?

    4. What did the word picture of those turned away at the gate of heaven bring to mind for you?

    5. Where do you want to be "from" in the eternal future?

- **Chapter 7 – Amongst**

    1. Have you got "baggage" you need help unloading?

    2. Are there any "false gods" competing with the One True God for your attention and service?

    3. Are you "self-centered" or "God-centered/other-centered?"

    4. Are you losing your life for Christ and others?

    5. Are you a good fragrance for Christ?

    6. Are you "toast" or an "heir with Christ?"

    7. Have you written down your testimony? Can you share it with others?

- **Chapter 8 – All**

  1. Are you or do you know any who are "cultural Christians?"

  2. Are you a sinner?

  3. How familiar are you with the Holy Scriptures – the Bible?

  4. Are you allowing the birds (of temptation) to build a nest in your hair?

  5. How is your morning devotional time?

  6. Are you asking Jesus what His plan for your life is?

- **Chapter 9 – This**

  1. Are you spending meaningful time reading meaningful books?

  2. Are you availing yourself to be able to have a "transforming" of your mind?

  3. Are you looking for opportunities to share your faith with others?

  4. Is Jesus a stumbling block for you or is He your cornerstone?

  5. Are you getting better at wielding the Sword of the Spirit – the Bible?

- **Chapter 10 – Chaos**

  1. Do you feel there is chaos in our world today?

  2. Where do you think it comes from?

  3. Are you praying for our government?

  4. Do you feel our nation is getting what it deserves?

  5. Where do you think, we as a nation, are headed?

  6. What are you going to do about it?

- **Chapter 11 - !**

  1. What do you rejoice in?

  2. How is your time management?

  3. Have you made serious efforts to get to "know yourself?"

  4. Do you have a friend you can confide in and trust to let you know if you are "living the lie?"

  5. Have you asked Jesus to help you be transformed more and more into His image?

  6. Why are you here?

  7. Which Way Is Up?

RESOURCES

READING LIST

Celebration of Discipline by Richard Foster (I've read 4 times)- One of the most impacting books I've read – gives you insights on what it means to truly live a more disciplined life for Christ!

Spirit of the Disciplines by Dallas Willard (I've read 3 times)- Along the same lines as Foster's book.

Margin by Richard Swenson (I've read 3 times)- This book will absolutely give you pause about what you're doing with your life, and help you reevaluate what is really important in it!

Spurgeon's Sermons (10 volume set – 5 books) from Amazon. com (I've read around 3700 pages)- A Baptist preacher in London in the 1850's gives sermons that are tremendously relevant to our lives today! His sermons paint word pictures that have greatly increased my insight into what my Savior and Lord did for me!

Love for a Lifetime by James Dobson (I've read 3 times)- A must for those thinking about marriage and newlyweds up to 10 years.

Life Application Bible from Zondervan (look at Sam's for $36.00)(I've been reading 5-7 days/week for 26 years)

I Surrender by Patrick Morley (I've read 2 times)- Helps us to realize most people worship the God they want Him to be, not the God Who really is!

Man in the Mirror by Patrick Morley – Helps men evaluate who they are and how they can better be the spiritual head of their families

This Present Darkness by Frank Peretti – Read this book in 1986 and it gave me insight into the spiritual warfare that is probably going on around us each and every day – a real page turner!

When Sinners Say "I Do" by Dave Harvey – This book is a TEN STAR book! GET IT!

Living the Cross-Centered Life by C.J. MaHaney – Tremendous book on living out the life God wants you to live!

Knowing God by J.I. Packer – I've read twice and is a "classic!"

In Pursuit of Man by A.W. Tozer – A short "classic"

In Pursuit of God by A.W. Tozer – Another short "classic"

The Attributes of God by Arthur Pink – Excellent!

Living Your Strengths by Winseman, Clifton, & Liesveld – Includes an online test that takes about 30 minutes to take and gives you instant results and insights as to why you do the things you do! GET IT!

MARK'S SCRIPTURE REFERENCES

1. Proverbs 1:7 – Are we fools? Or wise?
2. Proverbs 3:5-6 – Who do you trust – you or God?
3. Jeremiah 29:11-13 – God has a plan for your life!
4. Romans 7:4, Ephesians 2:10 – Why are we here?
5. 1 John 1:8-9 – We must confess our sins!
6. Joshua 1:8 – Meditate on God's Word daily!
7. 2 Timothy 3:16-17 – The Scriptures teach us.
8. Romans 3:20-31 – The "Heart" of the Gospel!
9. Revelation 3:20 – We must open the door!
10. Philippians 3:7-14 – Press-on to the upward call!
11. Galatians 2:20 – We have been crucified with Christ!
12. John 14:6, Acts 4:12, 1 John 5:11-12, 1Timothy 2:5 – Jesus is the ONLY way of salvation we have!
13. Romans 12:1-2 – Renewing of our mind transforms us.
14. Galatians 5:22-23 – The fruit of the Spirit, ask for it!
15. Matthew 6:25-34 – Do not worry!
16. Philippians 4:6-8 – Rejoice and don't be anxious!
17. Philippians 4:11-13 – Be content in everything!
18. Romans 5:1-5 – At the end of all suffering is hope!
19. Romans 8:28 – In all things, God works for the good!
20. Romans 8:37-39 – Nothing can separate us from Christ!
21. Psalms 1, 22, 23, 27, 51, 53, 69, 73, 91, 103, 111, 119, 138, 139
22. Hebrews 11 – The "Faith" chapter
23. Matthew 5-7 – The Sermon on the Mount
24. Ephesians – We believers are the body of Christ!
25. Ephesians 1:4 – God chose us!
26. Ephesians 2:8-9 – We are saved by grace!
27. Psalm 119:67-72, 105 – God's Word is a lamp to our feet!
28. Proverbs – The book of Wisdom!
29. 1 Corinthians 1:18 – The foolish perish!
30. Philippians 2:3-11 – Be an humble servant!
31. 1 Peter 2:9-10 – We as Christians are a royal priesthood!
32. 1 Peter 2:24 – Jesus Christ bore our sins!
33. 1 Peter 5:6-10 – God restores us!
34. Matthew 22:37-40 – The two great commandments!
35. Matthew 7:21-23 – One of the scariest verses in the Bible–Not all who think and say they are Christians are going to heaven!
36. Matthew 25:21 & 34 – The words we all long to hear!
37. Colossians 1:10-12 – My prayer for you!
38. Colossians 2:8 – Do not be deceived!
39. 1 Thessalonians 4:13-5:11 – Will you be left behind?
40. Matthew 25:31-46 – Eternal punishment vs. Eternal life in heaven – we will all be at one or the other!
41. 1 Thessalonians 5:16-18 – Thou shalt not BELLYACHE!
42. 2 Thessalonians 1:8-10 – Jesus – the ONLY way to avoid destruction!
43. John 3:35-36 – Eternal life with Jesus or God's wrath – which will you receive?
44. 2 Thessalonians 2:9-12 – Some will be deceived and perish!
45. Romans 1:20 – We are without excuse!
46. John 14:15, 21, 23 – If we love Jesus, we obey Him!
47. Isaiah 55:8-9 – God's thoughts and ways are higher than ours!
48. Hebrews 7:24-25 – Jesus intercedes for His saints!
49. John 17 – The Holy of Holies!
50. Matthew 10:32-33 – Don't be ashamed of Jesus!
51. Ephesians 6:10-18 – Put on the full armor of GOD!

**Intermedia
Publishing Group**

Publishing That Works For You

Do you need a speaker?

Do you want Mark Peters to speak to your group or event? Then contact Larry Davis at: (623) 337-8710 or email: ldavis@intermediapr.com or use the contact form at: www.intermediapr.com.

Whether you want to purchase bulk copies of *Which Way Is Up?* or buy another book for a friend, get it now at: www.imprbooks.com.

If you have a book that you would like to publish, contact Terry Whalin, Publisher, at Intermedia Publishing Group, (623) 337-8710 or email: twhalin@intermediapub.com or use the contact form at: www.intermediapub.com.